Poetry Place Anthology

More than 600 poems for all occasions!

Poems to celebrate each season and holiday. Poems to inspire zingy, zany art projects, bright, bold bulletin boards, creative dramatics, and original verse writing. Poems to remember long ago; to capture the spirit of today; to dream of things to come; and much, much more!

Instructor Books

Scholastic Inc., 2931 East McCarty Street, Jefferson City, MO 65102

ISBN: 0-590-49017

12   9/9

Printed in the U.S.A.
First Scholastic printing, September 1990

Instructor Books expresses its appreciation to the publishers and authors listed in "Acknowledgements" for their kind permission to print the poems in this book.

The content of this book is taken from materials published in Instructor magazine and Teacher magazine.

This book was compiled and edited by Rosemary Alexander and INSTRUCTOR staff: Susan Gaustad, assistant editor; and Loren Simmons, permissions assistant. Artist and designer: Charles Cary.

Contents

Summer Poems

Anytime Poems

Enjoying and Creating Poetry

Introduction

For as long as INSTRUCTOR magazine has existed, it has published poetry for classroom use. In each issue teachers have found a ready source of quality poems to share with their children. Over and over teachers have asked whether the poetry published in those issues had ever been collected in an anthology. This is that long awaited anthology. It is a collection of verse that has appeared in INSTRUCTOR magazine during the last 25 years.

The poems can serve many purposes—some will help you celebrate the seasons and holidays; many will introduce children to good literature and help them appreciate rhythm, meter, and rhyme; others will motivate writing and other creative activities. They express many moods, from joy and exuberance to melancholy, from seriousness to high humor.

Instructor Books hopes that you and your children will enjoy this *Poetry Place Anthology* and make many of its verses a part of your daily curriculum.

Acknowledgments

Lilian Moore, "Look at That!" in *See My Lovely Poison Ivy*. Copyright © 1975 by Lilian Moore. Reprinted with the permission of Atheneum Publishers. X.J. Kennedy, "Wicked Witch Admires Herself," in *The Phantom Ice Cream Man: More Nonsense Verse*. Copyright © 1979 by X.J. Kennedy. A Margaret K. McElderry Book. Reprinted with the permission of Atheneum Publishers. Patricia Hubble, "Our Washing Machine," in *The Apple Vendor's Fair*. Copyright © 1963 by Patricia Hubble. Reprinted with the permission of Atheneum Publishers. "Be My Non-Valentine" and "A Cliché" from *It Doesn't Always Have to Rhyme*, by Eve Merriam (Pat Ayers, agent), copyright © 1964 by Eve Merriam. Reprinted by permission of Pat Ayers. "Hurry" from *Out Loud*, by Eve Merriam (Pat Ayers, agent), copyright © 1973 by Eve Merriam. Reprinted by permission of Pat Ayers. "Our Flag" by Betty Scott Baker. Reprinted by permission of the author. "When We Drove Through a Tunnel" by Virginia Baldridge. Reprinted by permission of the author. "Necks," "The Raccoon," and "Skyscrapers" by Rowena Bennett. Reprinted by permission of Kenneth C. Bennett, Jr. "Memorial Day Parade" by Blanche Boshinski. Reprinted by permission of author. "Wilbur and Orville Wright" by Stephen Vincent Benet from: *A Book of Americans*, Holt, Rinehart and Winston, Inc. Copyright, 1933, by Rosemary and Stephen Vincent Benet, copyright renewed © 1961 by Rosemary Carr Benet. Reprinted by permission of Brandt & Brandt Literary Agents, Inc. "Miss Jones" and "Discovery" from *The Golden Hive*, by Harry Behn, copyright © 1962 by Harry Behn. Reprinted by permission of Curtis Brown, Ltd. "City Blockades" and "Naughty Donna" from *Charlie's World: A Book of Poems*, by Lee Bennett Hopkins, copyright © 1972 by Lee Bennett Hopkins. Reprinted by permission of Curtis Brown, Ltd. "The Museum Door," by Lee Bennett Hopkins, copyright © 1973. Reprinted by permission of Curtis Brown, Ltd. "Winter Reading" appeared in *The Christian Science Monitor* Feb. 3, 1962. Reprinted by permission of *The Christian Science Monitor*. "City Child" from *We Live in the City*, by Lois Lenski, copyright © 1954 by Lois Lenski. Reprinted by permission of Stephen Covey and Messrs. Covey. "Burdock the Warlock" by Wendy Mary Cruse. Reprinted by permission of the author. "My Mother," reprinted with permission from the book *Christopher O!*, by Barbara Young, copyright © 1947. Published by David McKay Co., Inc. "The Toaster" and "Dictionary" excerpted from the book *Laughing Time* by William Jay Smith. Copyright © 1953, 1955, 1956, 1957, 1959, 1968, 1974, 1977, 1980 by William Jay Smith. Reprinted by permission of Delacorte Press/Seymour Lawrence. "Chestnut Stands" from *Taxis and Toadstools* by Rachel Field. Copyright © 1926 by Doubleday & Company, Inc. Reprinted by permission of the publisher. "December" by S. Vanderbilt from *Creative Youth* by Hugh Mearns. Copyright © 1925 by Doubleday & Company, Inc. Reprinted by permission of the publisher. "Uncle Frank" from *Goose Grass Rhymes* by Monica Shannon. Copyright © 1930 by Doubleday & Company, Inc. Reprinted by permission of the publisher. "Jump or Jiggle" by Evelyn Beyer and "There Are So Many Ways of Going Places" by Leslie Thompson from *Another Here and Now Story Book* by Lucy Sprague Mitchell. Copyright 1937 by E.P. Dutton & Co., Inc.; renewal, 1965, by Lucy Sprague Mitchell. Reprinted by permission of the publisher, E.P. Dutton, Inc. "Passing by the Junkyard" by Charles J. Egita. Reprinted by permission of the author. "The Tiniest Sound" (six lines) from *The Tiniest Sound* by Mel Evans, copyright © 1969 by Mel Evans. Reprinted by permission of the author.

Reprinted by permission of Farrar, Straus and Giroux, Inc. "Pumpkin" from *More Small Poems* by Valerie Worth, pictures by Natalie Babbitt. Text copyright © 1976 by Valerie Worth. "The First Memorial Day" and "Now December's Here" by Aileen Fisher. Reprinted by permission of the author. "Fireflies" from *Up the Windy Hill* by Aileen Fisher, copyright © 1953 by Abelard Press, copyright renewed 1981 by Aileen Fisher. Reprinted by permission of the author. "Big Laugh" from *Chuckles and Grins* by Lee Blair, copyright © 1968 by Lee Blair. Reprinted by permission of Garrard Publishing Co. "Jumping Rope" from *Playtime in the City* by Lee Blair, copyright © 1971 by Lee Blair. Reprinted by permission of Garrard Publishing Co. "Race" by B.J. Lee, from *Playtime in the City*. Reprinted by permission of Garrard Publishing Co. (Selected by Leland B. Jacobs.) "First Day of April," "Without a Trumpet," "With a Friend," "A Pickle Is Long," and "At Hanukkah" all by Vivian Gouled. Reprinted by permission of the author. "Sleeping Silent" by Barbara M. Hales. Reprinted by permission of the author. "A Time for Building" from *Wide Awake and Other Poems*, copyright © 1959 by Myra Cohn Livingston. Reprinted by permission of Harcourt Brace Jovanovich, Inc. "Waiting" from *The Little Hill* by Harry Behn, copyright © 1949. Reprinted by permission of Harcourt Brace Jovanovich, Inc. "Paper I" from *The Complete Poems of Carl Sandberg*, copyright © 1950. Reprinted by permission of Harcourt Brace Jovanovich, Inc. "Day Is Done" from *Merrily Comes Our Harvest In* by Lee Bennett Hopkins, copyright © 1978. Reprinted by permission of Harcourt Brace Jovanovich, Inc. "Subway Rush Hour" by Langston Hughes, from *Montage of a Dream Deferred*, copyright © 1951. Published by Henry Holt, Inc. Reprinted by permission of Harold Ober Assoc. Inc. "I Like It When It's Mizzly" from *I Like Weather* by Aileen Fisher (Thomas Y. Crowell, Publishers). Text copyright © 1963 by Aileen Fisher. Reprinted by permission of Harper & Row, Publishers, Inc. "Freckles" from *In One Door and Out the Other* by Aileen Fisher (Thomas Y. Crowell, Publishers). Copyright © 1969 by Aileen Fisher. Reprinted by permission of Harper & Row, Publishers, Inc. "Rosh Hashanah" and "First Thanksgiving" from *Skip Around the Year* by Aileen Fisher (Thomas Y. Crowell, Publishers). Copyright © 1967 by Aileen Fisher. Reprinted by permission of Harper & Row, Publishers, Inc. "Love" from *Where the Sidewalk Ends*. The Poems & Drawings of Shel Silverstein. Copyright © 1974 by Shel Silverstein. Reprinted by permission of Harper & Row, Publishers, Inc. "Nobody Loves Me" from *All that Sunlight* by Charlotte Zolotow. Reprinted by permission of Harper & Row, Publishers, Inc. "Cynthia in the Snow" and "Tommy" from *Bronzeville Boys and Girls* by Gwendolyn Brooks. Copyright © 1956 by Gwendolyn Brooks Blakely. Reprinted by permission of Harper & Row, Publishers, Inc. "Circus" from *Eleanor Farjeon's Poems for Children* by Eleanor Farjeon (J.B. Lippincott, Publishers). Copyright © 1926, 1954 by Eleanor Farjeon. Reprinted by permission of Harper & Row, Publishers, Inc. "Spider Webs" from *A World to Know* by James S. Tippett. Copyright © 1933 by Harper & Row, Publishers, Inc. Renewed, 1961 by Martha K. Tippett. Reprinted by permission of the publisher. "Sitting in the Sand" and "Lewis Has a Trumpet" from *Dogs and Dragons, Trees and Dreams, A Collection of Poems by Karla Kuskin*. Copyright © 1958 by Karla Kuskin. Reprinted by permission of Harper & Row, Publishers, Inc. "Snowy Benches" and "Back to School" from *Out in the Dark and Daylight* by Aileen Fisher. Copyright © 1980 by Aileen Fisher. Reprinted by permission of Harper & Row, Publishers, Inc. "Little Seeds We Sow in Spring" from *The Winds That Come From Far Away and Other Poems* by Else Holmelund Minarik. Copyright © 1964 by Else Holmelund Minarik. Reprinted by permission of Harper & Row, Publishers, Inc. "Ferryboats" from *Crickery Cricket! The Best Loved Poems of James S. Tippett*. Originally published in *I Go A-Traveling* by James S. Tippett. Copyright © 1929, by Harper & Row, Publishers, Inc. Renewed, 1957, by James S. Tippett. Reprinted by permission of the publisher. "The Hippopotamus" by Georgia Roberts Durston from *Highlights for Children*, April, 1969, copyright © 1969. Reprinted by permission of Highlights for Children, Inc., Columbus, Ohio. "Merry-Go-Round," "One More Time," "Snowfall" and "Self-Starting" by Margaret Hillert. Reprinted by permission of the author. "Winter Fun" by Catherine Y. Hoagey. Reprinted by permission of the author. "The Subway Train" by Leland B. Jacobs, from *In Somewhere Always Far Away*, copyright © 1967. Reprinted by permission of Holt, Rinehart & Winston, Inc. "One Day When We Went Walking" by Valine Hobbs from *The Horn Book*. Reprinted by permission of Horn Book, Inc. "Ski Lift" by Ethel Jacobson. Reprinted by permission of the author. "Things to Do If You Are a Subway" by Bobbi Katz. Reprinted by permission of the author. "Lawn Mower" and "Merry-Go-Round" from *I Like Machinery* by Dorothy Baruch. Reprinted by permission of Bertha Klausner International Literary Agency, Inc. "Lincoln Monument: Washington," "April Rain Song," and "Dreams" from *The Dream Keeper and Other Poems*, by Langston Hughes. Copyright 1932 by Alfred A. Knopf, Inc., and renewed 1960 by Langston Hughes. Reprinted by permission of the publisher. "Winter Moon," copyright 1926 by Alfred A. Knopf, Inc., and renewed 1954 by Langston Hughes. Reprinted from *Selected Poems of Langston Hughes*, by permission of the publisher. "America Is on the Move," "October Is for Me," "That Christmas Feeling," "My Calendar," "The New Year," "Millions of People," "The Zipper," "Typewriter Song," "Instant Everything," "Winter Worries" all poems by Jane W. Krows. Reprinted by permission of the author. "Spelling Bee" from *Take Sky* by David McCord, copyright © 1961, 1962 by David McCord. Reprinted by permission of Little, Brown and Company. "Celery" by Ogden Nash, copyright © 1941. Reprinted by permission of Little, Brown and Co. "March," reprinted with permission of Macmillan Publishing Co., Inc., from *Summer Green* by Elizabeth Coatsworth. Copyright 1948 by Macmillan Publishing Co. Inc., renewed 1976 by Elizabeth Coatsworth Beston. "Summer Rain," reprinted with permission of Macmillan Publishing Co., Inc., from *Summer Green* by Elizabeth Coatsworth. Copyright 1940 by Macmillan Publishing Co., Inc., renewed 1968 by Elizabeth Coatsworth Beston. "An Explanation of the Grasshopper," reprinted with permission of Macmillan Publishing Co., Inc., from *Collected Poems* by Vachel Lindsay. Copyright 1914 by Macmillan Publishing Co., Inc., renewed 1942 by Elizabeth C. Lindsay. "High Flight" by Pilot Officer John Gillespie Magee, Jr., R.C.A.F. Permission to reprint by Mrs. John G. Magee. "Who" by Lilian Moore from *Little Raccoon and Poems From the Woods*, copyright © 1975. Reprinted by permission of the author. "Pirate Wind" by Mary Jane Carr from *Top of the Morning*, copyright 1941, renewed 1968, published by Thomas Y. Crowell Co. Reprinted by permission of McIntosh and Otis, Inc. "Winter Poem—3 Feb. 72" in *My House* by Nikki Giovanni. Copyright © 1972 by Nikki Giovanni. By permission of William Morrow & Company. "South Wind" by Kenneth Rexroth from *One Hundred Poems From the Chinese*, copyright © 1971. Reprinted by permission of New Directions Publishing Co. "On the Merry-Go-Round" by Bonnie Nims. Reprinted by permission of the author. "United Nations Day" reprinted by permission from United Nations Plays and Programs, by Aileen Fisher and Olive Rabe. Copyright © 1954 by Aileen Fisher and Olive Rabe. Plays, Inc., publishers, Boston. "When the Merry-Go-Round Is Still" by Anita E. Posey. Reprinted by permission of author.

Reprinted by permission of The Putnam Publishing Group: "Is Only Known" and "Kick a Little Stone" from *Before Things Happen* by Dorothy Aldis, copyright © 1937 by Dorothy Aldis; renewed 1967 by Mary Cornelia Aldis Porter; "Is Only Known" and "Kick a Little Stone" from *All Together* by Dorothy Aldis, copyright 1925, 1928, 1934; copyright renewed 1953, 1956, 1962 by Dorothy Aldis. "What They Are For" from *All Together*, copyright © 1952. Reprinted by permission of G.P. Putnam's Sons. "Everybody Says" from *All Together*, copyright © 1953-1956, 1962, 1967. Reprinted by permission of G.P. Putnam's Sons. "When Spring Came" (Tlingit Song) from *The Turquoise Horse* by Flora Hood, copyright © 1972 by Flora Hood. Reprinted by permission of The Putnam Publishing Group. Prince Redcloud for "Now." Used by the author who controls all rights. "Bird in the Hand," by Lee Avery Reed. Reprinted by permission of the author. "A Year Later," reprinted by permission of Russell & Volkening, Inc., as agents for the author. Copyright © 1959 by Mary Ann Hoberman. "I Like You" by Masuhito is reprinted from *I Like You, and Other Poems for Valentine's Day*, selected by Yaroslava, with the permission of Charles Scribner's Sons. *I Like You and Other Poems for Valentine's Day*, copyright © 1976 by Yaroslava Surmach Mills. "Father of the Future" by Ilo Orleans. Reprinted by permission of Karen S. Solomon. "Spring Cleaning" and "Windy Word" by Jean Conder Soule. Reprinted by permission of the author. "Getting Back" and "City and Trucks" by Dorothy Brown Thompson. Reprinted by permission of the author. "For Hanukkah" by H.N. Bialik, from *Far Over the Sea*. Copyright © 1939. Reprinted by permission of Union of American Hebrew Congregations. "School's the Pied Piper" by Maurine Wagner. Reprinted by permission of author. "Freckles" by Mabel Watts. Reprinted by permission of the author. "Sing a Song of Summer" and "Runny Nose" by Kay Winters. Reprinted by permission of the author. "Christmas Tree" by Aileen Fisher. First published in *Weekly Reader*, December 6, 1967. Copyright © *Weekly Reader*, 1967. Reprinted by permission. "Bundles" from *Songs for Parents* by John Farrar, copyright © 1921. Reprinted by permission of Yale University Press. "Parade" by Ruby Zagoren. Reprinted by permission of Samuel Silverstein.

Fall

Welcome the fall season with poems celebrating back to school, signs of autumn, and crisp October days. Check here for that just-right poem for Columbus Day, UN Week, Halloween, Veterans Day, Children's Book Week, and Thanksgiving.

BACK TO SCHOOL

When the summer smells like apples
and shadows feel cool
and falling leaves make dapples
of color on the pool
and wind is in the maples
and sweaters are the rule
and hazy days spell lazy ways,
it's hard to go to school.

But I go!

Aileen Fisher

SEPTEMBER

September is a lady
In a russet gown;
She marches through the country;
She marches through the town;
She stops at every schoolhouse
And rings a magic bell;

She dances on each doorstep
And weaves a magic spell.
She weaves a magic spell that goes
Winging through the land
And gathers children back to school
In a joyous band.

Solveig Paulson Russell

GETTING BACK

Coming back to school again—
All our crowd together—
What a lot of ways we've been
In many kinds of weather!
After all our journeyings,
We see familiar faces
And show each other all the things
We've brought from different places.

Jack has thrilling tales he tells
Of trails and mountain-reaches;
Constance has a box of shells
And agates from the beaches;
Mary saw the Capitol
From corner stone to dome;
And Jim has camera shots of all
His summer hikes at home.

Talking, laughing, looking out
To greet the latest comer—
We may finish, but we doubt
Our getting through till summer!
We must hear it all—we must
See each stone and feather—
And the best of all is just
Getting back together!

Dorothy Brown Thompson

SCHOOL'S THE PIED PIPER

School's the Pied Piper
    Calling boys and girls by name;
    September roll call.

Maurine Wagner

SCHOOL

Today we stood beside Corot
And saw the sunlight on the trees;
In high-built Spanish galleons
We sailed across the western seas,
Past strange and lonely islands whose
Inhabitants were cockatoos;

We walked through Hiawatha's land
And helped him build his birch canoe;
We peeped into a robin's nest
To see the eggs all smooth and blue;
And yet there are some folks who think
That school is only books and ink!

Blythe Cleave

A SCHOOL PRAYER

Now happy school days once again
Have brought us work and play,
And I am going to try to work
And play in the best way.

So every morning when I wake,
I'll start the day quite right
By thanking God for His great love
And care all through the night.

I'll ask God then to be with me
Through every hour of day,
To make me careful in my work,
And fair and true in play,

To bless each one I love at home,
And all my school friends, too,
And make each day a happy day
For all, the whole year through.

Monica Williams

SCHOOL AGAIN!

Oh, I am so excited, for
  September's come again;

I'm always glad, no matter how
  Much fun the summer's been.

My books are new, my pencils, too;
  My lunch is in my box.

It's such a lark to join my friends
  And go to school in flocks.

My hair is combed, my face is clean;
  Just hear that school bell ring!

Vacation's gone, but I don't care.
  I'm happy as anything.

Marian Stearns Curry

FRIENDSHIP'S RULE

Our teacher says there is a rule
We should remember while at school,

At home, at play, whate'er we do,
And that's the rule of friendship true.

If you would have friends, you must do
To them the kindly things that you

Would like to have them do and say
To you while at your work and play.

And that's the rule of friendship true;
It works in all we say and do.

It pays to be a friend polite,
For friendship's rule is always right.

M. Lucille Ford

SCHOOL

School bells are ringing, loud and clear;
Vacation's over, school is here.

We hunt our pencils and our books,
And say goodby to fields and brooks,

To carefree days of sunny hours,
To birds and butterflies and flowers.

But we are glad school has begun,
For work is always mixed with fun.

When autumn comes and the weather is cool,
Nothing can take the place of school.

Winifred C. Marshall

SOUNDS

I like the sound of many things—
Of tinkling streams, a bird that sings,
Of falling raindrops, buzzing bees,
Of crunching snow, and wind in trees.

I like the sound of happy play,
Of echoes soft and far away,
Of music gay or sweet and slow,
Of trains and cars that swiftly go.

But there is one sound nicer far
To me than all these others are;
I like the sound September brings
When once again the school bell rings.

M. Lucille Ford

LONELY DAY AT THE ZOO

The albatross was very cross,
The parrots were not funny,
The bears would not sit up and beg
Or even eat their honey.

The monkeys didn't chatter much,
The lion wasn't roaring,
The seals were swimming lazily,
The elephant was snoring.

"I wonder where the children are,"
The keeper said with sorrow.
He thought a bit and then exclaimed,
"Oh! School begins tomorrow!"

Helen M. Webster

NOW THAT I CAN READ

I used to need somebody
To sit and read to me.
I'd look at every page they read
And listen carefully.

But now that I am in first grade,
I'm filling up a shelf
With stories, poems, and other books
That I can read myself.

Ruth Etkin

HURRY

Hurry! says the morning,
Don't be late for school!

Hurry! says the teacher,
Hand in papers now!

Hurry! says the mother,
Supper's getting cold!

Hurry! says the father,
Time to go to bed!

Slowly, says the darkness,
you can talk to me....

Eve Merriam

LEARNING

Last year when I was little
    I could only count to three.
And never could remember
    What the next number should be!
But now that I've grown bigger
    I know more than I did then,
For I have been in school a month—
    And I can count to ten!

M. Lucille Ford

ROSH HASHANAH

"Come!" sounds the shofar,
"Come!" sounds the horn,
"Come with self-searching—
a new year is born.

"Think of the old year:
Have you been just?
Thoughtful of others?
Worthy of trust?

"Come!" sounds the shofar,
vibrantly clear,
"Come with self-searching
to greet the New Year."

Aileen Fisher

AUTUMN

When the trees their summer splendor
   Change to raiment red and gold,
When the summer moon turns mellow
   And the nights are getting cold;

When the squirrels hide their acorns,
   And the woodchucks disappear;
Then we know that it is autumn,
   Loveliest season of the year.

Charlotte L. Riser

SEPTEMBER

When the goldenrod is yellow
And leaves are turning brown—
Reluctantly the summer goes
In a cloud of thistledown.

When squirrels are harvesting
And birds in flight appear—
By these autumn signs we know
September days are here.

Brierly Ashour

IN AUTUMN

They're coming down in showers,
The leaves all gold and red;
They're covering the little flowers,
And tucking them in bed.
They've spread a fairy carpet
All up and down the street;
And when we skip along to school,
They rustle 'neath our feet.

Winifred C. Marshall

GOLDENROD

A blaze of yellow glory,
   The goldenrod in bloom;
Like a knight of olden story,
   It flaunts a feathery plume.

Fannie Montgomery

AMERICAN HERITAGE

The Declaration of Independence,
The Constitution with its Bill of Rights:
These are the bulwarks of our heritage,
These are our nation's guiding lights.

Freedom of speech, freedom of press,
Freedom to worship as we please,
The right to assemble, the right to petition,
Are some of the freedoms we recite with ease.

The right to life, the right to liberty,
The right to pursuit of happiness,
The right to equality, the right to security,
The right to live without undue stress.

But what of the many other rights,
Not written in our laws;
The right to labor, the right to suffer,
The right to fight for freedom's cause?

For these are rights our forefathers chose,
When they laid our country's foundation,
And these are the rights we must assume
To preserve our precious nation.

Elsie Walush

11

LEAF BLANKETS

Leaves are falling, soft as snowflakes,
　　Red and yellow, gold and brown;
The breeze laughs gaily in the treetops,
　　Shaking all the color down.

Leaves are covering the gardens
　　As my blanket covers me.
When cold winter comes, the flowers
　　Will be warm as warm can be.

Irene B. Crofoot

THE GIFTS OF AUTUMN

Autumn is hazy
　　And brilliant and dry.
Its deep blue burns
　　In the heavy sky.

Autumn is lavish
　　With frosted nuts
And purple grapes
　　Where the high field juts

Against the wood.
　　Autumn tumbles down
A wealth of color
　　On country and town,

A riot of leaves,
　　A harvest of fruit,
And stalk and seed
　　And berry and root.

And then when the sudden
　　Twilight falls,
Autumn's best gift
　　Is between four walls—

A blazing fire
　　And a kitten near
And popcorn and apples
　　And stories and cheer!

Revah Summersgill

AUTUMN WEALTH

Golden leaves aflutter,
　　Floating down from trees,
Golden sunshine tangled
　　With each passing breeze,
Golden glow in gardens,
　　Goldenrod in fields;
What a wealth of beauty
　　Autumn always yields!

Alice Hoffman

AUTUMN MEMORIES

For my autumn memories
　　I'll choose goldenrod,
A spray of purple asters,
　　A fuzzy milkweed pod,
A dahlia proud and stately,
　　A maple leaf so red,
A bunch of grapes, an apple,
　　And a lowly teasel head.

Leland B. Jacobs

AUTUMN

Cornflake leaves
Beneath the trees—
Are they a breakfast
For the breeze?

Thelma Ireland

THIS IS THE FALL

Grapes in the vineyard,
　　Purple and dark;
Brown leaves are floating
　　Down in the park.

Red are the apples,
　　Plenty for all.
This is the harvest,
　　This is the fall.

God gives us beauty;
　　God gives us food.
God gives us all things
　　Peaceful and good!

Nona Keen Duffy

CHESTNUT STANDS

Oh, every fall the chestnut men
   Are out by park and street,
Frosty mornings, sunny noons,
   And nights of stars or sleet.

Little stands at every curb,
   Charcoal fires that glow,
And like a spell that sharp, strange smell
   Wherever feet may go.

Smokey bitterness of leaves
   Burning who knows where?
Spicy scent of frost-nipped fruit
   Tingling on the air.

Town-dull folk might never guess,
   Or country hearts recall,
If chestnut men forgot to come
   To cities in the fall.

Rachel Field

WHOOO?

The wind is a wanton,
The wind is a tease
With no shame at all
Stripping the trees—
   When he comes blowing.

Watch out for the scamp;
Beware of the flirt;
Tie down your bonnet;
Hold fast to your skirt—
   When he comes blowing.

Eileen Burnett

PIRATE WIND

The autumn wind's a pirate,
   Blustering in from sea;
With a rollicking song, he sweeps along,
   Swaggering boist'rously.

His skin is weather-beaten;
   He wears a yellow sash,
With a handkerchief red about his head,
   And a bristling black mustache.

He laughs as he storms the country,
   A loud laugh and a bold;
And the trees all quake and shiver and shake,
   As he robs them of their gold.

The autumn wind's a pirate,
   Pillaging just for fun;
He'll snatch your hat as quick as that,
   And laugh to see you run!

Mary Jane Carr

SUMMONS

Some geese fly high;
Some skim low;
Across the sunset,
Ready to go.

When the moon rises
They will flock
Across the face of
Autumn's clock.

Eileen Burnett

AN AUTUMN DAY

Pumpkins in the cornfields,
Gold among the brown,
Leaves of rust and scarlet
Trembling slowly down;
Birds that travel southward,
Lovely time to play;
Nothing is as pleasant
As an autumn day!

Carmen Lagos Signes

OCTOBER

October is a gypsy queen
In dress of red and gold.
She sleeps beneath the silver moon
When nights are crisp and cold.

The meadows flame with color now,
Which once were cool and green.
Wild asters and the goldenrod
Bow low to greet their queen.

When she is tripping through the wood
With song so clear and sweet,
The autumn leaves come sifting down,
And rustle 'neath her feet.

Winifred C. Marshall

OCTOBER

October! October!
   There's magic in the name—
A clear sky, a blue sky,
   And sunsets all aflame.

October! October!
   It's harvest time again;
The high corn, the low corn,
   Is gathered in the bin.

October! October!
   Sing birds with open throats;
A long song, a last song,
   Of tender parting notes.

October! October!
   The hills are all aglow
With red leaves, and gold leaves,
   That dance when soft winds blow.

October! October!
   I love you more each year;
Your warm days, your soft days,
   To me they are most dear.

D. Maitland Bushby

OCTOBER IS FOR ME

October is the best of all
   In the fall.
Colored leaves come tumbling down,
   On the ground.

Footballs flying in the air,
   Everywhere.
School bands with their colors high,
   Marching by.

Wieners roasting in the wood,
   Smell so good.
Every season has its glory;
   That's the story.

But October is for me,
   Everything a month should be.
Haunting skies and haunting sounds;
   Haunting colors all around.

Cool by night and warm by day,
   There could be no better way.
Wouldn't it be quite a thing,
   If October stayed around till spring?

Jane W. Krows

SONG FOR OCTOBER

I like the chill October nights,
   And bright October days,
I like the dancing bonfire lights
   And misty purple haze,

I like the boastful brigand breeze
That robs the meek, defenseless trees.

I like October's bright bouquet
   With sumac flares of red,
And goldenrod and asters gay
   In rich profusion spread.

No rival yet has nature planned
For fair October's wonderland.

Leland B. Jacobs

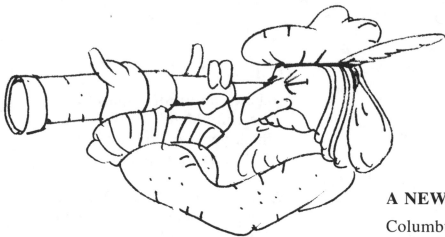

THE THREE SHIPS

The Niña, the Pinta, the Santa Maria,
  Three little ships from Spain,
Sailed over the seas, under skies so blue,
Sailed on through the wind and rain.
  So brave was the captain,
  So gallant his crew,
  Their faith remained steadfast
  Till their goal came in view.
The Niña, the Pinta, the Santa Maria,
  Three little ships from Spain,
Inspired the later pioneers
Who settled on hill and plain.
  So great was their labor,
  Their courage so true,
  That our mighty nation
  From their striving grew.

Lillian W. Allard

LIKE COLUMBUS

Columbus said, "The earth is round.
Across the sea I'll go.
Although some say the earth is flat,
I'll prove it is not so."

Columbus crossed the ocean. When
His sailors cried, "Turn back!"
He would not listen to their pleas,
But kept the onward track.

Then when Columbus sighted land,
Their cries and fears were gone.
I hope that I shall be as brave
As he was, and "sail on!"

Eleanor Dennis

A NEW WORLD

Columbus found a new world
  Because he dared to do
A thing that was unheard of—
  A thing that was quite new.

Columbus found a new world
  Because he made a start,
Instead of merely pond'ring o'er
  The thoughts within his heart.

Columbus found a new world
  Because he saw things through—
And you can find your new world
  Precisely that way, too.

Alice Crowell Hoffman

CHRISTOPHER COLUMBUS

Columbus was a wise man
  Who thought the earth was round;
He planned to sail across the sea
  Where trading could be found.

Though kings did not believe in him,
  And men thought he would fail,
He found one friend, the Spanish queen,
  Who gave him ships to sail.

The crew rebelled, the sea was rough
  In 1492;
Still this brave man kept sailing on
  In spite of sea or crew.

But when they spied America,
  They landed with a cheer—
And that is why we celebrate
  Columbus Day each year.

Gertrude M. Robinson

NO WASH, JUST WEAR

A squirrel, it seems, is always dressed
In all his velvet Sunday best.
(His suit of brown or gray or black
Fits snugly round his tail and back.)
Or are they really working clothes—
I guess nobody really knows.

I'm sure his mother doesn't care
Because his suit's "No Wash, Just Wear."
And if his feet get wet, you see,
He dries them on the nearest tree.
It might be nice to be a squirrel,
Instead of just a boy or girl.

John A. Kriebel

CRICKET SONG

The leaves are falling one by one,
And all the earth says, "Summer's done."
All cricket eggs are tucked away
For hatching on a bright spring day,
And now it's almost time to go
To find a niche safe from the snow,
But first I'll sing this farewell song,
In praise of summer warm and long,
Filled with joy and cricket bliss
That I am glad I didn't miss.
"I'm glad for summer's moonlit nights
When I could feed on plant delights,
And for my hole deep in the ground
Where rest and comfort could be found.
I sing farewell to those good days,
And to kind Autumn's friendly ways.
I sing farewell to summer fun—
Goodbye, goodbye to everyone."

Solveig Paulson Russell

TIME TO PLAY

A rabbit said to Mr. Squirrel,
  One chilly autumn day,
"I think you are quite foolish
  To hide those nuts away."

"Oho! my friend," said Mr. Squirrel,
  "The cold winds soon will blow,
And nuts will all be hidden
  Deep under drifts of snow.

"Now that is why I'm working
  With all my strength today;
When winter comes, I'll doubtless
  Have time enough for play."

Ada Clark

LITTLE SQUIRREL

A little squirrel runs up and down
  In our old walnut tree.
All day he carries nuts away,
  As busy as can be.
Mother says he stores them safe
  For food when north winds blow;
I wonder how the squirrel knows
  That some day there'll be snow.

Ethel Hopper

SQUIRRELS

Some little red squirrels
Live up in a tree,
Out in the woodland gay.
They frisk and frolic,
And scamper about,
On each bright autumn day.

But they are not idle;
They're working away,
Busy as they can be,
Filling a storehouse,
For long winter days,
Thrifty and wise, you see.

Winifred C. Marshall

BEAR WEATHER

Streams froze solid; ground did, too.
Bare trees shook in the wind that blew.
Snowflakes danced and fluttered and fell.
Folks all said, ''A long cold spell.''
But the big brown bear
And the small brown bear
Just didn't care.
They didn't care at all, at all;
They didn't care at all.

Windows were shuttered; fires grew brighter.
Folks all shivered, wrapped clothes tighter.
Barometer dropped; temperature fell.
Folks all said, ''A long cold spell.''
But the big brown bear
And the small brown bear
Just didn't care.
They didn't care at all, at all;
They didn't care at all.

Snug and warm in their deep, dark den,
Cuddled up close with cheek to chin,
They never knew the weather out there,
And they didn't care.
The big brown bear
And the small brown bear
Just didn't care.
They didn't care at all, at all;
They didn't care at all.

Lillie D. Chaffin

MR. OWL

I saw an owl up in a tree,
I looked at him, he looked at me;
I couldn't tell you of his size,
For all I saw were two big eyes;
As soon as I could make a dash,
Straight home I ran, quick as a flash!

Edna Hamilton

THE OWL AND THE WIND

Oh, did you hear the wind last night
    A-blowing right at you?
It sounded just as though it said,
    ''Oooo—ooo—oooo!''

The wind now has a playmate,
    Just as most children do,
He sits up in a tree and hoots,
    ''To-whoo, to-whit, to-whoo.''

So when you hear the owl and wind
    Just at the close of day,
They're calling to each other
    To come out now and play.

Madeline A. Chaffee

TWO BABY OWLS

Two baby owls sat in a tree,
And blinked because they could not see.
''The sun is shining bright,'' they said,
''So let's go home and go to bed.''

A little squirrel, frisking near
The owls, was very quick to hear.
Said he, ''It's fine for work or play;
I'm glad the sun shines bright today.''

Ada Clark

THE FLAGS OF THE UN

The flags of the UN
Are marching by;
Their colors are blazing
Beneath the sky.
And they whisper, ''Peace,
May it never cease.''

They are red, they are yellow,
They are green, they are blue.
They blend in a banner
Of myriad hue.
While they whisper, ''Peace,
May it never cease.''

There are flags from the New World,
There are flags from the Old,
The tropics, the Orient,
And Arctic cold.
And they whisper, ''Peace,
May it never cease.''

Jean Brabham McKinney

FRIENDS

As around the earth we go,
Mountain high and valley low,
River deep and desert wide.
Children are the same inside!

Skins are different, this we know—
White or black or copper glow.
Games we play and work we do,
Homes and schools, are different, too.
But we wish and hope and wonder.
We are all the same down under!

Oh, how fine if we could be
Friends, with hands across the sea,
Boys and girls of one great world.
Look! The UN flag's unfurled!

Margaret B. Brown

UNITED NATIONS DAY

This is the birthday of a hope.
This is the birthday of a plan.
This is a day of breadth and scope
in the adventuring of man.

This is a planet-wide event,
not just a date in scattered lands.
Humbly, in every continent,
this is a day men lift their hands.

This is the birthday of a trust
that peace will not be lost again.
This is the birthday of a *must* . . .
this is the birthday of UN.

Aileen Fisher

FACE TO FACE

I'd like to go around the world
And get a chance to see
The boys and girls of other lands
And let them all see me.

I'd like to meet them face to face,
And get to know their names.
I'd like to sit and talk with them
And learn to play their games.

I'd like to visit in their homes,
Their family life to share.
I'd like to taste the food they eat,
And see the clothes they wear.

I'd like to get to know them well
Before my journey's end;
For only when you know someone
Can he become your friend.

And so, someday, I'd like to go
Around the world and see
The boys and girls of other lands
And let them all see me.

Anita E. Posey

HALLOWEEN FUN

Tang of cider in the air,
Spooks and goblins everywhere,
Caldrons bubbling in the night,
Jack-o'-lanterns burning bright
Gypsies stirring steaming brew.
On the fences black cats mew.
Bats in darkened corners hide.
Lurid witches broomsticks ride.
Skulls and crossbones act as hosts
To rows and rows of stately ghosts.
   That's Halloween!

Fern Curtis

LOOK AT THAT!

Look at that!
Ghosts lined up
at the Laundromat,
all around the
block.
Each has
bleach
and some
detergent.
Each one seems to
think it
urgent
to take a spin
in a
washing machine
before the
clock
strikes
Halloween!

Lilian Moore

19

IT'S HALLOWEEN

Strange things happen
  on Halloween night.
A witch sails by on a broom.
Pumpkins grin slyly
  from rickety fences
As owls fly away to the moon.

Virginia P. Flanagan

HALLOWEEN PALS

A happy little fellow
sat on my fence one night
His smile was full and wide—
A most amazing sight!

He said to me, "I'm yours for keeps.
I hope you'll like me fine.
I've watched you now,
for weeks and weeks
while growing on my vine.

Just put me in your window
when the right time rolls around.
I promise that I'll glow for you
And never make a sound.
I'll be your friend forever.
We'll be happy as can be.
For I'm your jack-o'-lantern,
And you're just right for me!"

Jeanne Morger

HALLOWEEN

Witches, ghosts, and bats are seen
out at night on Halloween.
Boys and girls with scary faces
peer out from many spooky places.
Everything looks very queer
this jack-o'-lantern time of year!

Ruth Linsley Forman

THREE GHOSTESSES

Three little ghostesses,
Sitting on postesses,
Eating buttered toastesses,
Greasing their fistesses,
Up to their wristesses,
Oh, what beastesses
To make such feastesses!

Anonymous

ON HALLOWEEN NIGHT

Let's fly like a bat
On Halloween night.
And give all our neighbors
A terrible fright!
Or creep through the dark
Like a big, black cat.
And make all our neighbors
Cry, "What was that?"
Or float like a ghost
In the dark midnight air,
And make everyone run
And hide to beware.
Then maybe tomorrow
When the witching hour's done,
We'll give in and tell them
It was Halloween fun!

Ruth Linsley Forman

A GOOD DISGUISE

"I'm going to dress myself so queer
For Halloween," I said, "this year,

Nobody else will ever guess
That I am little Mary Bess."

I put my old clothes all in place,
I fastened on my funny face,

Looked in the glass above the shelf,
And didn't even know myself!

Alice Crowell Hoffman

A HALLOWEEN WISH

If I could borrow a witch's broom,
　I'd ride far above the town;
I'd see the place where the sun comes up,
　The place where the moon goes down.

I'd fly around by the old church tower
　And wave to the folk below;
I'd see the haunts of the wise night owl
　And follow the fireflies' glow.

I shouldn't care for a tall black hat
　Or cat with fiery eye—
But I'd like to borrow a magic broom
　And fly as the witches fly.

Mabel Harmer

A TALE OF HALLOWEEN

It was Halloween night
And there on the grass
In a large, cozy ring
All the jack-o'-lanterns sat
When out of the woods
Stepped three witches with brooms
Followed by a hissing black cat.

One witch lit a fire
And into a pot
Stirred snake root with a silver spoon.
When the cat took a drink
Of this horrible brew
He was rocketed straight to the moon.

The witches shrieked
And did a weird dance,
Then off on their brooms went spinning.
The fire went out
And there on the grass,
All the bright jack-o'-lanterns sat grinning.

Virginia P. Flanagan

BURDOCK THE WARLOCK

Burdock is a warlock;
a warlock of renown.
His sorcery and magic spells
are famous in his town.
And the witches all adore him
for his culinary arts—
They rave and crave for Burdock's
famous jellyfish tarts.

But that's not all that Burdock cooks.
Oh, no! He makes a stew
that makes the witches' tongues hang out
and some their eyeballs, too.
The main ingredients, you will note,
can be smelt for miles around:
Rotten eggs and sauerkraut
and toads minced up and ground.

Add to this some liverwort,
cankerworms and gnats,
two pig's feet, a dragonfly,
and fifteen tails of rats.
The witches come from miles around
just to smell his stew,
but the normal folk all disappear—
They cannot stand the PHEW!

Wendy Mary Cruse

A PUMPKIN SEED

A pumpkin seed's a little thing,
When it is planted in the spring,
But, oh, the fun that it can bring!

At Halloween it turns into
A pumpkin pie for me and you,
Or jack-o'-lantern that says "Boo!"

Alice Crowell Hoffman

THE PUMPKIN THAT GREW

One time there was a pumpkin,
And all the summer through
It stayed upon a big green vine,
And grew, and grew, and grew!

It grew from being small and green
To being big and yellow
And then it said unto itself,
"Now I'm a handsome fellow!"

And then one day it grew a mouth,
A nose, and two big eyes!
And so that pumpkin grew into
A jack-o'-lantern wise!

M. Lucille Ford

PUMPKIN

After its lid
Is cut, the slick
Seeds and stuck
Wet strings
Scooped out,
Walls scraped
Dry and white,
Face carved, candle
Fixed and lit,
Light creeps
Into the thick
Rind: giving
That dead orange
Vegetable skull
Warm skin, making
A live head
To hold its
Sharp gold grin.

Valerie Worth

UNHAPPY PUMPKIN

The pumpkin was unhappy, for
  He did not want to stay
Tied to a vine, beneath the corn,
  And never go away.

He wished he were the sun, so he
  Could roll around the sky.
"If I keep growing like him, I
  May get there by and by."

Though he grew big and yellow, he
  Was not the sun. Instead
He became a jack-o'-lantern
  With a candle in his head.

Louisa J. Brooker

POMPOUS MR. PUMPKIN

Pompous Mr. Pumpkin,
You needn't look so wise,
Perched upon a picket fence
Staring with your eyes—

Needn't think that I'm afraid
Of your fearful frown
Or your great big glaring teeth
Or your mouth, turned down;

Mr. Pumpkin, run from *you?*
No, sir—no, indeed—
Because I knew you long ago
When you were just a seed!

Elsie Melchert Fowler

THE JACK-O'-LANTERN

Billy brought a pumpkin in
And Mother scraped it out.
Daddy carved a little mouth
With such a funny pout.

Sally cut some crooked eyes
And trimmed the thing with beads,
While everybody laughed at me
Because I saved the seeds.

But I will plant them in the spring
And wait till fall, and *then*—
I'll have at least a hundred
Jack-o'-lantern men!

Florence Lind

TWO YELLOW PUMPKINS

Once there were two yellow pumpkins,
    Growing on a vine;
And they said to one another,
    "Aren't we just fine!
Wonder what to us will happen
    When we go from here,
Will we be turned to chariots golden
    And travel far and near?"

One day there came into the cornfield
    A little girl and boy;
Each one seized a yellow pumpkin,
    As though it were some toy.
Said Boy, "I'll make a jack-o'-lantern,
    Now won't that be great?
His face shall be so big and funny,
    He'll surely be first rate."

Said she, "I'll bake my yellow pumpkin
    Into a pie so nice;
Then let me share your jack-o'-lantern,
    And I'll give you a slice."
And so, that night when all was quiet—
    At least for Halloween—
They sat beside the jack-o'-lantern,
    With the golden pie between.

Blanche A. Steinhover

JACK-O'-LANTERN GARDEN

I wish I had a garden,
    Where the warm sun brightly shines.
I'd plant each nook and corner
    With jack-o'-lantern vines.

Then, from my little garden
    I'd pick for Halloween
More golden jack-o'-lanterns
    Than you have ever seen.

Of course, I'd choose the biggest,
    The one that's brightest gold,
To peep in at your window—
    Oh, there, I almost told!

Gertrude M. Robinson

PUMPKINS

A farmer grew pumpkins;
   So, late in the Fall,
He went out one day
   And he gathered them all!

The biggest and roundest
   He sent to the fair
In hopes of its winning
   A blue ribbon there.

The rest went to market,
   Except for a few;
His wife made some pies
   Of all except two.

And what of the two?
   Oh, they're a surprise
With long, jagged teeth
   And a light in their eyes!

Nona Keen Duffy

WICKED WITCH ADMIRES HERSELF

"Mirror, mirror on the wall,
Whose is the fairest face of all?
I'll come close, so you'll see me clearer—"

Pop! goes another magic mirror.

X.J. Kennedy

FUNNY FEAR

I don't like people to shout "BOO"
   When we are out at play;
I don't like to feel *shivery*
   On any other day,
But, somehow, creepy games are *fun;*
   I like to think I've seen
A witch or bat, queer things like that,
   When it is Halloween!

Frances Gorman Risser

JUST WONDERING

What becomes of the witches on broomsticks
The day after Halloween?
Does anyone know where the goblins go
Or why none of the ghosts are seen?
I wonder about those big black cats
And the owls that hooted at night.
I've asked around but yet haven't found
Why they've all disappeared from sight.
I still have my jack-o'-lantern
And his eyes look as wise as can be.
Now do you suppose that he really knows?
And is that why he's grinning at me?

Blanche Garretson

AUTUMN GHOST SOUNDS

When the moon
rides high,
up overhead—
and I am snug
and warm,
in bed—
in the autumn dark
the ghosts move 'round,
making their
mournful,
moaning sound.

I listen to know
when the ghosts
go by.
I hear a wail,
and I hear a sigh.

But I can't quite tell
which I hear
the most—
the wind,
or the wail
of some passing ghost.

Anonymous

ARMISTICE DAY VISION

I saw a cross upon a hill—
 A cross like some weird lily;
It marked the place a soldier lay—
 It made me creepy, chilly.

I saw a time beyond the cross
 When men no longer would
Wage war on one another—
 A time of brotherhood.

Alice Crowell Hoffman

HEROES WE NEVER NAME

Back of the men we honor
 Enrolled on the scroll of fame,
Are the millions who go unmentioned—
 The heroes we never name!
Those who have won us the victories,
 And conquered along the way;
Those who have made us a nation—
 A tribute to them I would pay.

Back of our nation's first leader,
 Of Lincoln and Wilson, too,
Back of the mind directing our course
 Was the army that carried it through.
Back of the generals and captains
 Was the tramping of rank and file,
And back of them were the ones at home
 Who labored with tear and with smile.

And what of the "everyday" heroes
 Whose courage and efforts ne'er cease!
Toilers who struggle and labor and strive
 And hope for a future of peace?
Hats off to the worthy leaders;
 Their honor I'd ever acclaim—
But here's a cheer for the many brave,
 The heroes we never name!

M. Lucille Ford

VETERANS DAY

Flags today in tribute wave
For those loyal ones who gave
Of their youth, their hopes, their might
For a cause they knew was right.

 Morning bells sound their call.
 Pause and say a prayer for all—
 All who served valiantly
 That men might be ever free.

 Taps from quiet Arlington
 Echo again.
 Ever keep in memory
 Peace-loving men,
 Who, hating tyranny,
 Struggled that liberty
 Should for all time be
 Won for every land.

Once again the challenge came,
And the answer was the same.
Eager hearts have made it clear
We would guard what we hold dear.

 Toll of bells, drums' slow beat—
 Silence falls in every street.
 In each heart swells the plea:
 Keep us safe, but keep us free!

Kate Englehardt Clark

WINTER READING

Wonderful things can happen when you read a book.
Snow can pile up quietly in the back yard.
Birds can make furry noises under the eaves.
Day can turn to dark as you turn the pages.
Cakes can be baked in the kitchen, and your nose can twitch.
Kittens can curl up at the back of your neck.
Little brothers can orbit the house and re-enter, with a bang.
Big sisters can drift out on their way to somewhere.
Fathers can sound contented under their daily papers.
New worlds can come and go with the turn of a chapter.
Winter can be green and sunny all of a sudden.
Wonderful things can happen while you read a book.

Edsel Ford

BOOKS ARE FOR LOOKS

Books are for looks; a look for a tale
Of possibly a lion, a tiger, or a whale.

A look for adventure, exciting, intense
With mystery unfolding and growing suspense.

A look for a fact, to inform or relate,
A picture, a poem, or a word to locate.

You never can tell when you start to look
What interesting things may come in a book!

Isabelle Spooner

I LIKE A BOOK

I like a book. It tells me things
Of ancient peoples and their kings
And what they used to do;
Of giants in some far-off land
And things I hardly understand,
Both make-believe and true.

I like books. It's fun to see
How interesting they can be—
As people are. And so
I try to treat them like a friend
And many pleasant hours spend
In learning what they know.

M. Lucille Ford

WHO HATH A BOOK

Who hath a book
Has friends at hand,
And gold and gear
At his command;
And rich estates,
If he but look,
Are held by him
Who hath a book.

Who hath a book
Has but to read
And he may be
A king indeed;
His kingdom is
His inglenook;
All this is his
Who hath a book.

Wilbur D. Nesbit

BOOKS

Books are friends who take you far
    Wherever you would go,
From torrid lands and jungle ways
    To northern fields of snow.

Books bring us gifts from long ago
    And hints of future days,
And lead the mind refreshingly
    On unfamiliar ways.

Books are the chests of pirate gold
    Where wealth in stories lies
As varied as the clouds that blow
    Across November skies.

Solveig Paulson Russell

MAGIC KEYS

Would you like to travel far
From the place where now you are?
   Read a book.

Would you nature's secrets know,
How her children live and grow?
   Read a book.

Is it adventure that you crave,
On land or on ocean wave?
   Read a book.

Would you like to talk with kings?
Or to fly with Lindbergh's wings?
   Read a book.

Would you look on days gone by?
Know scientific reasons why?
   Read a book.

The world before you will unfold,
For a magic key you hold
   In a book.

   Leah Gibbs Knobbe

MY STORYBOOK

While Puss curls at my feet to dream
Of fat, fat mice and bowls of cream
I like to sit for hours and look
Through my favorite storybook.

I read about the strangest things:
Wild animals that talk, and kings,
Lost princesses, and hidden gold
And birds, and elves, and pirates bold.

There's nothing I like more to do;
And though 'tis sad, yet it is true,
It seems to me I've never read
Enough when I must go to bed!

   Elaine V. Emans

READING BOOKS

I like to read all kinds of books
To entertain myself,
And so I'm glad when I can take
A book down from the shelf.

I like the picture books of planes,
Of flowers, birds, and ships
From which I can imagine that
I'm taking wonder trips.

I like the books with stories in
And also books of rhymes;
I often try to learn a few
And say them lots of times.

I like to read *all* kinds of books
I find upon the shelf—
Particularly now that I
Can read all by myself!

   Vivian G. Gouled

MY BOOK

My book and heart
Shall never part.

   Old Rhyme

AN ADVENTURER

I relive each deed
Whenever I read
Of the past ages
In my history pages!

I cross desert sands
And visit strange lands;
I explore every sea
In geography!

And I am a knight
Wearing armor bright,
Whenever I look
In my storybook!

   Elaine V. Emans

THANKSGIVING DAY

Brave and high-souled Pilgrims, you who knew no fears,
How your words of thankfulness go ringing down the years;
May we follow after; like you, work and pray,
And with hearts of thankfulness keep
Thanksgiving day.

Annette Wynne

BOOKS

Books
Lead folks
To other lands.
Books
Bind folks
With friendship's bands.
Books
Tell folks
Of bygone days.
Books
Bring folks
Tomorrow's ways!

Eileen Burkard Norris

GOING TO THE LIBRARY

I walk inside a building where
  The children's room I see,
With pretty books all round about—
  They're waiting there for me.

Bright flowers are painted on the walls,
  And story folks I know,
Who live inside the books I read—
  All round the room they go.

I take my book, and then I find
  A table with a chair.
I want to read about a knight
  Who saves his lady fair.

I'm in a pirate ship at sea;
  I'm hunting buffalo.
Oh, anywhere I open books,
  Adventuring I go.

Ella Waterbury Gardner

ADVENTURES WITH BOOKS

Books are ships
That sail the seas
To lands of snow
Or jungle trees.
And I'm the captain bold and free,
Who will decide which place we'll see.
Come, let us sail the magic ship.

Books are trains
In many lands,
Crossing hills
Or desert sands.
And I'm the engineer who guides
The train on its exciting rides.
Come, let us ride the magic train.

Books are zoos
That make a home
For birds and beasts
Not free to roam.
And I'm the keeper of the zoo,
I choose the things to show to you.
Come, let us visit in a zoo.

Books are gardens
Fairies, elves,
Cowboys, and people
Like ourselves.
And I can find with one good look
Just what I want, inside a book.
Come, let us read! For reading's fun.

Velda Blumhagen

GLAD THANKSGIVING DAY

November days are cheerful
Though frost is in the air,
For it's then that nature gives us
Her gifts for all to share.

Her gifts for all to share,
And so we store away,
But best of all we love it
For glad Thanksgiving Day.

The golden corn is gathered,
The bins are running o'er,
The cellar's full to bursting
With such a goodly store.

With such a goodly store,
All treasured there it lay,
And so we praise the Giver
For glad Thanksgiving Day.

Effie Crawford

FIRST THANKSGIVING

Venison for stew and roasting,
oysters in the ashes toasting,
geese done to a turn,
berries (dried) and wild grapes (seeded)
mixed with dough and gently kneaded—
what a feast to earn!

Indian corn in strange disguises,
ash cakes, hoe cakes (many sizes),
kernels roasted brown . . .
after months of frugal living
what a welcome first Thanksgiving
there in Plymouth town!

Aileen Fisher

WERE YOU AFRAID?

Were you afraid, Pilgrim,
When you took leave of all you knew
To go across an ocean
Into a world unknown?
Were you afraid, Pilgrim,
When you saw the wild rough land
That didn't really welcome you,
And strange new people
Who stood and stared?
Were you afraid, Pilgrim,
In your white starched collar
And silver-buckled shoes,
Or did you know
That this was freedom's road?

Beryl Frank

THE MAYFLOWER

Across Atlantic waters drear,
Defiant of the winds that roar,

Through heavy seas it dared to steer
A fearless course to freedom's shore.

More precious than rare gems or gold,
Across the ocean's billowy foam

In safety came, deep in the hold,
The daily needs of hearth and home.

The tilting decks were bravely trod
By heroes of a faith sublime,

Who asked in daily prayers to God
For freedom in a foreign clime.

Throughout our nation's history,
This fearless ship will ever stand

A symbol of democracy,
A tribute to our Pilgrim band.

Leland B. Jacobs

GIVE THANKS

For all the blessings that are ours,
For all our food, for lovely flowers,
  Give thanks!
For trees that give us fruit to eat,
For winter cold and summer heat,
  Give thanks!

For Mother's love and Father's aid,
For all the wonders God has made,
  Give thanks!
For friends and toys with which to play,
For restful night, and joyous day,
  Give thanks!

Carmen Lagos Signes

A CHILD'S SONG

I'm thankful for the sunshine bright,
For rain and for stars at night;
I'm thankful for each flower and tree,
And all the beauty that I see.

I'm grateful for our singing birds
And for my mother's gentle words;
I'm grateful for kind friends and true;
Help me to be a good friend, too.

Alice F. Green

THANKSGIVING

The year has turned its circle,
The seasons come and go.
The harvest is all gathered in
And chilly north winds blow.

Orchards have shared their treasures,
The fields, their yellow grain,
So open wide the doorway—
Thanksgiving comes again!

Anonymous

A THANKSGIVING DINNER

Take a turkey, stuff it fat,
Some of this and some of that.
Get some turnips, peel them well;
Cook a big squash in its shell.

Now potatoes, big and white,
Mash till they are soft and light.
Cranberries, so tart and sweet,
With the turkey we must eat.

Pickles—yes—and then, oh, my!
For dessert a pumpkin pie,
Golden brown and spicy sweet.
What a fine Thanksgiving treat!

Maude M. Grant

DAILY THANKS

Everything on Grandpa's farm
  Makes known its gratitude
By giving, in some simple way,
  Its thanks for daily food.

When Grandpa feeds the chicks and hens,
  They gather round his feet,
And cluck to say they're thankful for
  The grain they have to eat.

The horses whinny when they're fed
  Which is their way to say
Their thanks for pails of golden oats
  And mangers of sweet hay.

If animals can find a way
  To show their gratitude
I'll not forget to say a prayer
  Of thanks for daily food.

Eunice Cassidy Hendryx

GRATITUDE

I have a box
Full of all kinds of blocks,
And a little toy wagon painted red;
And a ball to roll
And a bread-and-milk bowl,
And a soft pink blanket for my bed.

I have a silver spoon
And a purple balloon
And boots, when the rain rains hard;
And a Daddy and a Mommie
And a big brother Tommie,
And a sand pile in my yard—

Don't you think a child like me
Should very, very thankful be?

Josephine Van Dolzen Pease

FOR COMMON JOYS

Thanksgiving for each joyful song
We hear along the way,
For voices that are dear to us,
The birds' glad roundelay.

Thanksgiving for each beauty new
That greets our seeking eyes;
For the sunset's glow and the day's full cheer,
And every dawn's surprise.

Thanksgiving for the boundless love
That surges in on every side;
For blessings from the hand of God
And for the good that they provide.

Thanksgiving for each precious gift
Life brings and bids us treasure;
For common joys of every day,
For good things without measure
    Let us give thanks!

M. Lucille Ford

A THANKSGIVING PRAYER

I'm thankful that the world was made
  Big and wide and round,
So that there would be room on it,
  And space could still be found
For all the little children's homes
  To cuddle snugly down
Across the snowy countryside,
  In city and in town.

Alice Crowell Hoffman

SIGNS OF THANKSGIVING

There are pies all set away in rows
  Upon the pantry shelf;
And plum pudding in the cake box,
  Alone, all by itself.

There's mincemeat nice and spicy
  Stewing on the kitchen stove;
I know it's full of raisins,
  And cinnamon and clove.

There are pumpkins big and golden,
  Lying out upon the field,
And heaps and heaps of apples,
  All the orchard trees can yield.

There's a tangy, frosty sweetness
  Glowing in the autumn air,
And a kind of happy feeling
  Around 'most everywhere.

Out in the yard our turkey
  Is strutting all around,
Picking up the yellow corn
  That's scattered on the ground.

He doesn't seem to mind one bit,
  Although it's very clear
That he knows what is coming—
  Thanksgiving's almost here!

Frances Wright Turner

A THANKSGIVING FABLE

It was a hungry pussy cat, upon
  Thanksgiving morn,
And she watched a thankful little
  mouse, that ate an ear of corn.
"If I ate that thankful little mouse,
  how thankful he should be,
When he had made a meal himself, to
  make a meal for me!
Then with his thanks for having fed,
  and thanks for feeding me,
With all *his* thankfulness inside, how
  thankful I shall be!"
Thus mused the hungry pussy cat,
  upon Thanksgiving Day;
But the little mouse had overheard
  and declined (with thanks) to stay.

Oliver Herford

THE PINECONE TURKEY

Once a little pinecone turkey,
  With feathers stiff and hard,
Wished that he could gobble loudly
  Like turkeys in the yard.
They gobbled high, they gobbled low,
  They gobbled with a trill;
And the little pinecone turkey
  Could only keep quite still.

But when he stood on the table
  On last Thanksgiving Day,
And saw a big brown turkey there
  His heart was light and gay.
His heart sang high, his heart sang low,
  His heart sang with a trill;
And the little pinecone turkey
  Was glad he'd kept quite still!

Mabel Maurine Henderson

DAY IS DONE

We've eaten all our dinner,
prayed our prayers,
wished our wishes.

Now it's time to get to work
and wash up
all these dishes!

Lee Bennett Hopkins

A THANKSGIVING RIDE

Five jolly, fat pumpkins one moonlight night,
  Said, "Come, let us all take a ride;

The turkeys will take us, with ease and delight."
  So they all rode away in great pride.

But soon Mistress Cook cried out in dismay,
  "Oh, where are my turkeys and pies?"

"They all went away, to spend Thanksgiving Day,"
  Said the moon, laughing down from the skies.

Ella M. Powers

THE TURKEY'S OPINION

"What dost thou think of drumsticks?"
  I asked a barnyard bird.
He grinned a turkey grin, and then
  He answered me this word:

"They're good to eat, they're good to beat;
  But sure as I am living,
They're best to run away with
  The week before Thanksgiving."

Anna M. Pratt

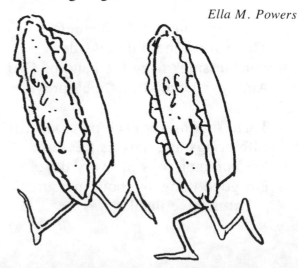

Winter

Use poetry to get in the spirit of winter weather and fun; to bring excitement to Hanukkah, Christmas, the New Year, and Valentine's Day; to honor our country's patriots—Lincoln, Washington, Franklin, Lee, Edison, Martin Luther King, Jr.

WINTER PLEASURES

What a wealth of jolly things
Good old winter always brings!

Ice to skate on, hills to coast—
Don't know which we like the most!

Games to play, and corn to pop—
Midnight seems too soon to stop!

Books to read aloud at night,
Songs to sing, and plays to write!

Snowmen built on starry nights,
Snow forts held in snowball fights!

High winds whirling drifted snow,
Breaths all frosty, cheeks aglow!

These and more, chill winter brings—
What a host of jolly things!

Nona Keen Duffy

WHO?

Who's been
criss-
crossing
this fresh snow?

Well, Rabbit was here.
How did he go?
Hop-hopping.
Stopping.
Hopping away.

A deer
stood near
this tall young tree.
Took three steps.
(What did she see?)
Didn't stay.
(What did she hear?)

Fox brushed snow dust
from a bush.
But who—
WHO
walked on TWO legs
here
today?

Lilian Moore

33

FOR HANUKKAH

Father lighted candles for me;
   Like a torch the Shamash shone.
In whose honor, for whose glory?
   For Hanukkah alone.

Teacher bought a big top for me,
   Solid lead, the finest known.
In whose honor, for whose glory?
   For Hanukkah alone.

Mother made a pancake for me,
   Hot and sweet and sugar-strewn.
In whose honor, for whose glory?
   For Hanukkah alone.

Uncle had a present for me,
   An old penny for my own.
In whose honor, for whose glory?
   For Hanukkah alone.

H. N. Bialik
Translated by Jessie Sampter

HANUKKAH QUIZ

Why is the story of Hanukkah told?
To honor the brave Maccabeans of old.
What makes our mouths water, handed around?
Platefuls of pancakes, deliciously browned.
Where are the Hanukkah gifts hidden?
   Well,
That is a secret which no one should tell!
What do we place on the table to hold
The gay-colored candles? It's polished gold.
The shining menorah!
What comes once a year?
Hanukkah fun!
At last it is here!

Eva Grant

JOYOUS HANUKKAH!

At last! At last! Hanukkah is here!
The whole house is bursting with holiday cheer.

Pancakes are sizzling as hard as they can,
Browning delectably crisp in the pan.

The dreidels can scarcely wait to be spun;
Presents are hidden for Hanukkah fun;

And there, on the table, polished and bright,
The shining menorah gleams through the night,

Like the oil lamp in ancient history,
That burned on and on miraculously!

And each flaming candle proclaims the great story
Of the Maccabean heroes, their deeds and their glory.

Eva Grant

AT HANUKKAH

Lighting Hanukkah candles
and watching them burn and glow;
Listening to the story
of Hanukkah long ago;
Giving and getting presents
each day, and that means eight . . .
Hanukkah is a happy time,
fun to celebrate.

Vivian Gouled

HANUKKAH HARMONICA

Last Hanukkah was the best—
full of stories and of laughter,
latkes, dreidels, candles bright,
shiny gelt. And then right after
we opened our presents, neatly wrapped:
a book from Mom, a shirt from Dad,
and from my cousin Monica
a wonderful harmonica!

I learned to play it right away,
took it with me everywhere—
played horas after Hebrew school,
played polkas for the Purim Fair,
played mayim for our Parents' Night,
played lullabies by campfire light.

I must take time out from this day
to write a note long overdue.
Here is what I want to say
(Don't you think that you would, too?):
"Dear cousin Monica,
I love the harmonica
You sent me last Hanukkah!"

Mimi Brodsky

HAPPY HANUKKAH!

Outside, snow is slowly, softly
Falling through the wintry night.
In the house, the brass menorah
Sparkles with the candlelight.

Children in a circle listen
To the wondrous stories told,
Of the daring Maccabeans
And the miracles of old.

In the kitchen, pancakes sizzle,
Turning brown, they'll soon be done.
Gifts are waiting to be opened,
Happy Hanukkah's begun.

Eva Grant

SONG OF HANUKKAH

Come and sing a Hanukkah song.
Sing of heroes, brave and strong—
Maccabeus and his band,
Who rescued Israel's ancient land.

Sing a song of candles burning,
Dreidel spinning, pancakes turning,
Hanukkah presents tucked away
To open on the holiday.

Sing a happy Hanukkah song
Every day for eight days long.

Eva Grant

FAMILY HANUKKAH

Mother's in the kitchen frying
Potato pancakes, crisp and light,
Father hides the children's presents
To be opened every night.
Amy shines the brass menorah
Till it glitters like the sun,
David counts the tiny candles,
He will light them one by one.
Grandma bustles round the household,
Then Grandpa joins the Hanukkah fun,
He tells the Maccabean story,
A family Hanukkah has begun!

Eva Grant

HANUKKAH RAINBOW

Eight little candles in a row,
Gaily colored,
All aglow.
Scarlet, purple,
Green, white, blue,
Pink and yellow,
Orange too.
The menorah,
Shining bright,
Holds a rainbow
Hanukkah night.

Eva Grant

WILBUR WRIGHT AND ORVILLE WRIGHT

Said Orville Wright to Wilbur Wright
''These birds are very trying.
I'm sick of hearing them cheep-cheep
About the fun of flying.
A bird has feathers, it is true.
That much I freely grant.
But must that stop us, W?''
Said Wilbur Wright, ''It shan't.''

. . .

And finally, at Kitty Hawk
In Nineteen-Three (let's cheer it!),
The first real airplane really flew
With Orville there to steer it!
—And kingdoms may forget their kings
And dogs forget their bites,
But not till Man forgets his wings,
Will men forget the Wrights.

Stephen Vincent Benet

FOREST FRIENDS

The gracious fir tree—
sparkly green and forest free—
keeps warm in winter's winds
with yearly added limbs.

Upon its outstretched arms,
and adding to its charms,
perch friends and neighbors fair—
some singles and then a pair.

All nestled close together,
keeping warm against the weather
they sing a heartfelt toast—
giving thanks to their friendly host.

Kate Eldridge

FIREWOOD

Sing a song of birchwood,
Cedar, oak and pine:
All the hearth is glowing bright,
All the room ashine.

Wind is in the chimney;
Snow is on the ground;
Kettle's singing very soft
With a cozy sound.

Sing a song of chestnut,
Hickory, and beech;
Firelight across the dark
As far as eye can reach.

Snow is on the forest;
The moon is icy cold;
But a lump of pitchwood
Will turn a room to gold.

Julia W. Wolfe

A WINTER INN

I know an inn that is safe and snug
    When wintry winds are blowing;
Its walls are thick, and its roof keeps out
    The cold when it is snowing.

The squirrels rent a little room
    When leaves blow helter-skelter,
And snowbirds wee come flocking there
    To share its welcome shelter.

The bright sun warms it through the day,
    And so it's never chilly,
Though breezes keen with icy breath
    Blow from the pastures chilly.

The spruces and the evergreens
    With needles thick and furry
Are inns to which, when cold winds blow,
    The wood-folk like to hurry!

Arthur Wallace Peach

CHRISTMAS IS A WARM THING

Christmas is a warm thing, wrinkled or new;
A softness and bright lights all red, green, and blue;
A tingle, a tiptoe, a fire aglow;
All crispy and nippy—a snowflake and snow.

Christmas is tinsel, a present, a tree;
A crying and laughter, a giggle of glee;
Or quiet, a candle, a flicker of flame;
A whisper, a touch—the soft falling rain.

Christmas is good folks, old, young, the same;
Visitors and carols again and again;
A pudding, a plum, a goose full of fat;
A smelling, a stuffing of this, those, and that.

Christmas is a shepherd, a journey, a stall;
A mother's wee baby—a gift to us all—
A reverence, a service, a towering spire;
A feeling, a surging, a triumphant choir.

Christmas is everything, poorest or bare;
Richly ornated, embraced with care;
A vision for all or one hope, set apart;
A tree thing, a real thing that lives in my heart.

Shirley Powell McPhillips

THAT CHRISTMAS FEELING

I feel Christmas in the air
Snowflakes falling everywhere:
Except in warm and sunny places
Where snowflakes never show their faces.
But everywhere the trees are trimmed
With twinkling lights on every limb.
They make the homes so gay and bright
And along dark streets shine out at night.
It is a season warm and glowing
Although outside it may be snowing.
Whether you live North or South
In mobile home or manor house,
You must feel Christmas in the air
And know it is a time to share.
And what a season to be jolly
With Christmas greens and Christmas holly.

Jane W. Krows

DREAMING OF CHRISTMAS

Have you heard the night wind sing,
  "Christmas is almost here!"
Have you heard the sparrows chirp,
  "Christmas is very near!"
Have you heard the hall clock tick,
  "Christmas is seconds away!"
Have you heard the reindeer hoofs?
  Wake up! It's Christmas Day!

Camilla Walch Knox

BUNDLES

A bundle is a funny thing,
It always sets me wondering:
For whether it is thick or wide
You never know just what's inside.

Especially in Christmas week
Temptation is too great to peek!
Now wouldn't it be much more fun
If shoppers carried things undone?

John Farrar

WHAT THIS COUNTRY NEEDS

The house is full of packages,
  Mysterious and gay,
But every one is labeled
  In the meanest sort of way.

"Do Not Open until Christmas!"
  'Most every label reads;
So I've come to the conclusion
  That what this country needs

Is someone to manufacture
  Some labels plain and bright:
"Open This Package When You Please."
  Now, don't you think I'm right?

Inez George Gridley

BUSY

Busy making popcorn balls,
  Busy with the tree,
Busy mailing greeting cards,
  Busy, busy me!

Busy wrapping packages;
  Say, I will be bound—
I'm so busy—I don't see
How Santa gets around!

Leland B. Jacobs

SHOPPING EARLY

I'll do my shopping early,
  This year at Christmas time.
I've saved my birthday dollars,
  Some quarters and a dime.

I have my list of presents
  All written out, you see.
Tomorrow I'll go shopping,
  And Jean will go with me.

It will be very pleasant,
  When Christmas Day draws near,
To know I need not hurry,
  The way I did last year.

Winifred C. Marshall

NOW DECEMBER'S HERE

Everything is "secrets"
now December's here:
Secrets wrapped in tissue,
whispered in an ear,
Secrets big and bulky,
secrets small and slight,
in the strangest places,
hidden out of sight.
Packages that rattle,
packages that squeak . . .
Some say, "Do not open."
Some say, "Do not peek."
Secrets, secrets, secrets,
with Christmas coming near.
. . . except it is no secret
I wish that it were *here.*

Aileen Fisher

WINDOW SHOPPING

Store windows during Christmas time
Hold treasures fine to see—
Gay drums and horns and jumping jacks,
And a doll just meant for me.

It's fun to stare and pick a toy
That we would like to take,
But there's so much to choose from
That the choice is hard to make.

So we leave it to Santa,
For he is wise, you see,
And knows what's best for all of us
To find beneath our tree!

Regina Sauro

CHRISTMAS IN THE CITY

Christmas in the city,
Crowds on every street,
Smiles on friendly faces,
Stamp of snowy feet.

Gay lights on the lampposts.
Bright trees everywhere,
Sounds of chimes and church bells
On the cold, crisp air.

Candles in the windows,
Smell of spruce and pine,
Stockings on the mantle,
Hanging in a line.

Jean Brabham McKinney

THE TWENTY-FOURTH OF DECEMBER

The clock ticks slowly, slowly in the hall,
And slower and more slow the long hours crawl;
It seems as though today
Would never pass away;
The clock ticks slowly, s-l-o-w-l-y in the hall.

Unknown

BEFORE CHRISTMAS

Young trees of the forest,
By scores and by dozens,
Have come to the city
Like small country cousins.

On squares and on corners
They lend to each street
A strange kind of fragrance
That's spicy and sweet.

So give them a welcome,
Be glad we are blessed
For even a season
With such sturdy guests.

They're waiting so gravely
The gay, joyous night,
When they will be dazzling
With color and light.

Anne Blackwell Payne

CHRISTMAS MAGIC

What a shining
   And Christmasy sight
Of hurrying crowds,
   And of windows alight!

Something of Christmas
   In everyday places,
Something of Christmas
   On all people's faces!

And on the corner,
   A Christmas-tree store
Where only the grocer's
   Was before!

J. Van Dolzen Pease

CAN YOU GUESS?

What's green and silver and happy and bright?
What's singing and loving and filled with light,
Gay and laughing wherever you go,
The friendliest, merriest time that we know?
Of course!
It's Christmas!

Georgia Deal

A SECRET

Do you know why the pine trees
   Stand so straight and tall,
Spread their branches thick and fine,
   And never stoop at all?

It really is a secret
   Which the North Wind told to me:
Every pine tree hopes some day
   To be a Christmas tree.

Laura Alice Boyd

CHRISTMAS PLANTS

Oh, the mistletoe and holly,
The bayberry and yew,
The needled pines and hemlocks,
And the fir trees, too,
All lend themselves at Christmastime
To make the season gay,
Shedding fragrance and cheer
In their own bright way.

The poinsettia adds its beauty,
And the yule log burns with cheer,
And other plants add to the fun
At the ending of the year.
So here's a cheer for Christmas greens,
And all plants that have a part
In making Christmas blossom
In the gardens of the heart!

Solveig Paulson Russell

SANTA UP-TO-DATE

My grandma tells how Santa Claus
   drove eight or ten reindeer,
And if you'd listen in the night,
   the sound of bells you'd hear;
Then, with his sleigh piled up so high
   you couldn't see the top,
He'd make his round of visits and
   no home was e'er forgot,
     In days of long ago.

Well, maybe reindeer were all right
   in days of long ago,
But in this day of "hurry-up" a
   reindeer is too slow.
So Santa has decided he will be up-
   to-date
And run no risks with reindeer that
   might get him 'round too late—
     So he flies an airplane now.

If ever I can see his airplane in the
   sky,
You bet I'll have my dad fix a good
   landing strip close by.
So 'stead of bells a-ringing, if you
   listen in the night,
You'll hear his engine roaring, and
   you'll know he's come all right—
     For he flies an airplane now.

Ada Rose Demerest

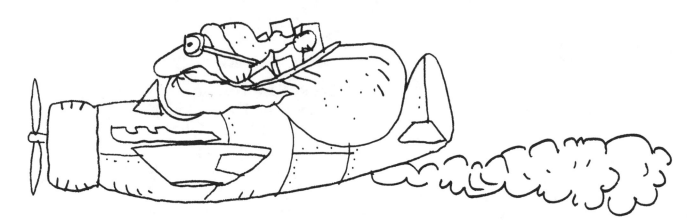

CHRISTMAS TREE

My kitten thinks
the Christmas tree
is more than something
just to see.

She taps the balls
of green and red,
and swings the tinsel
overhead,

And rings the bells,
and starts to purr
as if we'd trimmed it
all for her.

Aileen Fisher

HOLLY AND MISTLETOE

Holly and mistletoe,
   Candles and bells,
I know the message
   That each of you tells.

Ornament, tinsel, and
   Striped candy cane,
What you're suggesting
   Is perfectly plain.

Though you are silent,
   It's really quite clear
That you all are telling me
   Christmas is here.

Leland B. Jacobs

SANTA CLAUS AND COMPANY

In the still and frosty night
Stand the reindeer, poised for flight;
Their breath is seen on frosty air,
Their feet are restless, waiting there.

The sleigh is packed and riding low
In drifts of newly fallen snow;
Its bursting sides filled to the top
With toys to leave at every stop.

When Santa sashes through the door
With heavy pace, more gifts in store,
The reindeer strain, their stances taut,
The starlight in their harness caught.

With waves and shouts and gleeful "Hey"
Old Santa jumps into the sleigh;
And off they fly with breathless pace
To worlds below in boundless space.

Flying, flying, flying, climbing, climbing, climbing,
Sailing, sailing, sailing, drifting, drifting, drifting,
Over, under, through, and around
All the clouds, their path is wound.

This night their task is one of joy,
To bring to every girl and boy
Something wished for all the year
And now, in Santa's sleigh, so near.

Anticipation, palpitation, exhilaration, expectation!
All the "ations" in creation
Can't describe the great elation
Of Santa Claus and Company.

LaVonne Guenther

THE NEW YEAR

A glad New Year, each day a page,
   As fresh and white as snow;
Cold winter, and waking spring,
   And summer, warm and slow;
Bright autumn, jolly Halloween,
   Thanksgiving, Christmas cheer—
The record of a happy time,
   A beautiful New Year!

Margaret Oleson

THE NEW YEAR

A brand New Year arrived last night;
It came while I was waiting.
But I did not hear the horns or shouts
Of people celebrating.
Because, you see, I fell asleep
Before the hour, when
The old year silently passed out
And the New Year entered in.
But I have a clean new calendar
Which hangs before my eyes
And every day that's listed
Will hold a new surprise.

Jane W. Krows

MY CALENDAR

My calendar is fresh and new
And you will have a new one, too
For a brand new year has just arrived,
And each month will bring a new surprise.

Take **January;** it comes first
And sometimes is the very worst.
For we up North have fun and woe
With sleet and ice and heavy snow.
And **February,** short and sweet,
Brings valentines and candy sweet.
And then we take days off to praise
Dear George and Abe on their birthdays.
March brings us wind with which to fly
Our homemade kites across the sky.
With fickle March, you're never sure
If spring or winter will endure.
April, what a happy sound.
Spring rains and sunshine all around.
New flowers are holding up their faces
While birds are nesting in their places.
In **May,** the sun is really booming
And everywhere the flowers are blooming.
Around the maypoles children spin
And May baskets are carried to our kin.
In **June** vacation time comes around,
And also brides in bridal gowns.
You play and picnic in the park,
But hurry home when it is dark.

July's the month that really rates
With July Fourth to celebrate.
But July comes along so fast,
And half the year is already past.
August means school and fall are near.
Enjoy those days that are left, my dear.
And although the sun is very hot,
Just tan and swim and dive a lot.
September, schooltime once again,
So grab those books and just dig in.
The days are warm, the nights are fine,
And football is the big pastime.
October, month of gold-red trees;
Of wiener roasts and falling leaves.
We're getting out our warmer wraps.
And sometimes even wear our caps.
November, we can hardly wait
Thanksgiving Day to celebrate.
At Grandma's house we eat and cry,
"More turkey, dressing, and pumpkin pie."
December, wintry month with snow
Christmas lights and menorahs all aglow.
These holidays make a happy season
Peace and goodwill must be the reason.

And so the year has sped away,
And something new appeared each day.
So we prepare to watch again
The Old Year out, the New Year in.

Jane W. Krows

WHITE WITCH

Winter, the white witch, casts her spell.
The hedgerows, furred and stealthy, creep
Like snowy panthers to the well.
Almost they spring upon the sheep
That yesterday were pasture stones.
Wolves from the cedars came last night
To snarl among the gleaming bones
Of broken birch. The russet flight
Of red fox through the orchard burns;
And from the plumed grass, deep and warm,
The apple tree, defiant, turns
His antlered head against the storm.

Ruth Lechlitner

WITHOUT A TRUMPET

It blows
    without a trumpet.
It beats
    without a drum.
It whistles
    without a whistle,
Or it just
    begins to hum.

It sings or gently whispers,
Or it rages and it roars,
But . . . whatever kinds of noises . . .
Wind makes them outdoors.

Vivian Gouled

WINTER MOON

How thin and sharp is the moon tonight!
How thin and sharp and ghostly white
Is the slim curved crook of the moon tonight!

Langston Hughes

WINTERTIME

Late lies the wintry sun abed,
A frosty, fiery sleepyhead;
Blinks but an hour or two; and then,
A blood-red orange, sets again.

Before the stars have left the skies,
At morning in the dark I rise;
And shivering in my nakedness,
By the cold candle, bathe and dress.

Close by the jolly fire I sit
To warm my frozen bones a bit;
Or, with a reindeer-sled, explore
The colder countries round the door.

When to go out, my nurse doth wrap
Me in my comforter and cap;
The cold wind burns my face, and blows
Its frosty pepper up my nose.

Black are my steps on silver sod;
Thick blows my frosty breath abroad;
And tree and house, and hill and lake,
Are frosted like a wedding-cake.

Robert Louis Stevenson

WINTER NIGHT

Winter winds are blowing,
    Snow is drifting deep;
Cuddled under cover,
    Earth has gone to sleep.

Cozy in their houses
    Little children stay,
Where bright fires are burning
    To keep the cold away.

Snug in caves and burrows
    Wild things safe are curled,
While the feet of winter
    Tramp across the world.

Claude Weimer

43

FIRST SNOW

Mother Nature's dressmaker
Has been busy, that is clear;
I guess somebody told her
That wintertime was here,
I see that in the night she's brought
New clothing everywhere.
All the trees wear white fur
Which yesterday were bare,
And every post has a new hood,
Wooly white and high,
While on the roofs and in the fields
Thick snow-blankets lie.

I'm glad that old Dame Weather
Can meet all outside's needs
And clothe the barren branches
And cover sleeping seeds,
And I'm glad she makes her coverings
So beautiful and white
That Earth looks like a wonderland
Shimmering in the light.

Solveig Paulson Russell

SNOWFALL

Someone in the sky last night
Had an awful pillow fight,
And when I woke today I found
All the feathers on the ground.

Margaret Hillert

SNOWY BENCHES

Do parks get lonely
in winter, perhaps,
when benches have only
snow on their laps?

Aileen Fisher

A WINTER SURPRISE

Last night while I was sleeping
   The snow came softly down
And slipped on all the shrubbery
   A shining snowflake gown.

I guess that every little bush
   Felt startled with surprise
To find itself a cotton plant
   On opening up its eyes.

Solveig Paulson Russell

CYNTHIA IN THE SNOW

It SUSHES.
It hushes
The loudness in the road.
It flitter-twitters,
And laughs away from me.
It laughs a lovely whiteness,
And whitely whirs away,
To be
Some otherwhere,
Still white as milk or shirts.
So beautiful it hurts.

Gwendolyn Brooks

44

A CRYSTAL OF SNOW

A crystal of snow is a wonderful thing
With texture as fine as a butterfly's wing;
With network of atoms like filmy spun lace,
Or petal arrangement of fair flower face.

A crystal of snow is a beautiful thing
With the sparkle of drops that to spiders' webs cling
On a bright dewy morn; and the luster of pearl;
Or a diamond gleam on a glistening curl.

A crystal of snow is a curious thing—
With dew of summer—or rain of spring—
And frost of autumn mixed into it all;
The flowers of cloudland that earthward do fall.

M. Lucille Ford

I WONDER

A snowflake landed on my nose,
  And slid a little way;
Another followed, then a third
  Joined them without delay.

More snowflakes followed, thick and fast,
  And slipped down, side by side
I wonder if they thought my nose
  Was a toboggan slide?

Frances Gorman Risser

SPARKLING SNOW

The steps were covered,
The sidewalks were, too;
The roof tops were gone
Except for the flue;

The bushes were there,
Just humps on the ground;
The grass was certainly
Nowhere to be found;

The little twigs quivered
On each willow tree,
And swayed back and forth
And threw feathers at me.

The window was covered
With fluffy white flakes
Like frosting on one
Of my best birthday cakes.

O what a delight
To awaken today
And see sparkling white snow
In which to play.

Helen Kitchell Evans

WINTER POEM

once a snowflake fell
on my brow and i loved
it so much and i kissed
it and it was happy and called its cousins
and brothers and a web
of snow engulfed me then
i reached to love them all
and i squeezed them and they became
a spring rain and i stood perfectly
still and was a flower

Nikki Giovanni

ICICLE

Icicle is the strangest
Fruit from fairyland
    It tastes like—nothing!
    It goes to nothing
      In my hand.

Charlotte Mann

RUNNY NOSE

It's just not funny
When your nose is runny;
You feel all soggy,
Hoarse and froggy.
Your throat is scratching;
The germs are hatching.
You know it's catching—
KERCHOOO!

Kay Winters

WINTER WRAPS

The pine tree wears a jaunty cap
    Of snowflakes white, today;
The fir tree wears a fluffy suit
    That makes him look quite gay;

The leafless maple, sheathed in ice,
    Is stylish as can be,
But I am snuggled in the coat
    My mother made for me!

Frances Gorman Risser

DECEMBER

A little boy stood on the corner
And shoveled bits of dirty, soggy snow
Into the sewer—
With a jagged piece of tin.

He was helping spring come.

Sanderson Vanderbilt

SPIRALS OF SILVER

Silvery icicles—sharp and brittle
    March 'round the roof-edge, big and little
      One thin spiral curves at the end
        Because chilly North Wind made it bend

No two are alike as they sparkle and shine
    In icy perfection—a dazzling design
      In winter's white cold, they've nothing to fear
        'Til warm, sunny days when they'll all disappear!

Lorraine M. Halli

ICE

Ice
    is nice
      when you're straight
        as a willow,
But
    much too hard
    to use
      as a pillow.

Lou Ann Welte

THE SNOWPLOW

I'm standing by the window,
In my bathrobe of blue,
Watching the snowplow
Coming through;
Watching it 'way down the street.
Men lean on their shovels
And watch it too.

The plow moves forward;
Then it retreats
Moves forward again,
And then repeats.
I like to watch
The game it plays.
The snowplow has
Such funny ways.

Women rush out
For their garbage pails;
Dogs are barking
And chasing the trails
Of snow the snowplow sifts
As on it comes,
Turning the drifts.

I like to see it
Move forward, retreat,
Go forward again,
And then repeat,
Closing the driveways
But clearing the street.
It's fun to watch the city crew
And the snowplow coming through.

Florence Edick Sullivan

THE TINIEST SOUND

I used to think
the tiniest sound in the world
might be a baby snowflake
leaving a little white cloud
to drift gently down
through a misty sky

Mel Evans

SNOW STARS

Delicate
And feathery,
Crystal clear
And white,
Six-point stars
Come tumbling,
Softly
In the night.

Regina Sauro

SNOWY DAY

A snowy day has a special grace—
Flakes whirling,
Softly swirling,
Lightly floating,
Whitely coating
Every leafless woodland bower.
Willow stumps along the lake
Are frosted like a wedding cake.
How magically made, each flake
Patterned lovely as a flower
Or a star,
Falling far
From a burdened cloud!
Every twig and branch is bowed
With petals of this airy stuff,
This delicate, this fairy stuff—
Scudding, skipping,
Dancing, dipping,
Flakes caress my upturned face.
A snowy day has a special grace!

Ethel Jacobson

CLAIRE IN WINTER

The eyes are Claire's, and the nose is too,
But the feet are red rubber, the hands woolly blue.
The hair's covered up by a stocking cap,
And each little ear is beneath a flap.
Claire has a waist as slim as a fiddle;
This child is four yards around the middle!
There are leggings, petticoats, a bright plaid skirt.
There's a lot of snow, and a little dirt.
There's a coat and sweater, a blouse trimmed with lace.
There are socks and shoes, each one in its place.
And when the clothes are all neatly piled
There in the center I find a small child.
It's like peeling an onion, is undressing Claire,
And sometimes I wonder if she will be there,
Or if underneath the mountains of clothes
I'll find a stranger nobody knows.
Or worse still, undress her only to find
The clothes have come home and left Claire behind!

Margaret O. Slicer

THE FIREPLACE

In summertime
The fireplace
Just sits and stares
Without a face,
But in the fall
The sun gets weak,
And the fireplace
Begins to speak.
It snaps its fingers
And wiggles its toes
And roars with laughter
When we tickle its nose.

Liz Stoffel

BRING ME AN APPLE

Bring me a bright red apple to hold,
To hold on this winter night,
When all of the outside world is white
And the little apple tree sleeps in the cold.
Bring me its firm, round fruit;
And you will have brought me essence and root,
All that is summer: white petals drifting,
Leaves looking up to the sun,
Clouds cherry-colored, with daylight done,
Rain in the branches and cool wind lifting
A song in the little tree.
Bring me an apple. Bring summer to me.

Elsie McKinnon Strachan

WINTER WORRIES

Oh, lucky, lucky, lucky me!
I'm lucky as a child can be.
When winter winds my ears would harm,
My fuzzy earmuffs keep them warm.
When ice and snow take little nips,
Warm mittens cover finger tips.
My cozy coat keeps out the breeze,
My corduroys protect my knees.
But, up to now, no clothes are sold
To keep my *nose* from getting cold!

Jane W. Krows

SNOWY SIDEWALK

We watched our walk fill up with snow.
  It looked so soft and smooth!
And then the paper boy rode by
  And gave our walk a groove!

Mabel Pool

PICTURE

Today the forest
glistens white,
silvered with snow
that came last night.
The paths are gone,
no rabbits stir;
the only sound's
a scarlet whir
of cardinal wings
lifting high
into the blue
of winter sky.

O.J. Robertson

CRUMBS ON THE SNOW

When it's winter and the snow
Like a tablecloth is spread,
I remember hungry birds
And see that they are fed.
On their snowy tablecloth
They find my gift of bread.

Lucretia Penny

WAITING

Dreaming of honeycombs to share
With her small cubs, a mother bear
Sleeps in a snug and snowy lair.

Bees in their drowsy, drifted hive
Sip hoarded honey to survive
Until the flowers come alive.

Sleeping beneath the deep snow
Seeds of honeyed flowers know
When it is time to wake and grow.

Harry Behn

THE NEW OUTFIT

"I wish," said Willie Weasel, "that
I had a different coat and hat.
I'm awfully tired of wearing white;
I want a coat that's not so light."

"My gracious!" said his mother then,
"You'll get a nice brown outfit when
The new spring styles are on display,
But not upon this snowy day."

"I want it now. I hate to wait
Till such a long and far-off date."
So said wee William with a frown,
"It's brown I want; I want brown!"

Next morning when wee Willie woke,
His brothers thought it quite a joke
To find his wish had now come true;
A suit he had both brown and new!

Then Willie capered up and down,
And weasels eyed him, toe to crown.
What! Could springtime be so near?
It must be coming soon this year.

He scampered quickly to the wood,
Though Mother hadn't said he could.
"I'll show my friends a thing or two.
I'm sure they haven't suits so new!"

And then around the corner came
Old Slinky Coyote after game.
Poor Willie stood quite petrified
And hoped the snow would help him hide.

But his brown coat stood out so well
That Slinky spied him in the dell!
And then you should have seen them race
Back through the woods to Willie's place.

Poor Willie's heart thumped pitapat,
But Slinky stumbled and fell flat.
So Willie did get home all right;
Though suffering badly from the fright.

Now Willie must stay home awhile
Until brown suits are *ALL* in style.

Audrey McKim

WINTER WORLDS

Our cedars are steeples of snow.
    Our shrubs are mounds of ice.
But under them, to and fro
    Go partridges and mice.

With crystal roofs and walls
    Their crisscrossed tunnels lead
To cosy dens and halls
    And storerooms stocked with winter feed.

What softly pattering feet
    Scurry unseen below
Our world of ice and sleet,
    Our land of steepled snow!

Ethel Jacobson

WINTER GUESTS

Hurrah! for the bravest birds of all!
They did not fly away last fall.
They do not mind the ice and snow,
but sing a song when north winds blow.
Fire-red cardinal; junco gray;
and rusty sparrow and jaunty jay;
the chickadee in a white vest—
I love these winter birds the best.

Oh, peanut butter on crumbs of cake
and treats of suet balls I make,
and seeds of sunflowers by the score
I heap on their feeders outside my door
to bid them welcome, every one,
And keep them strong for the winter fun.
Few winter guests are as bright as these—
cardinals, bluejays, and chickadees.

Elsie S. Lindgren

I KNEW WHO YOU WERE

I saw your tracks
but I didn't see you
and I wondered where
you were—
I kept as still
as still could be
but there wasn't
a single stir.

I guess you must
have gone straight home
and I wanted to follow
you there—
for I'd like to know
just what you do
and how live
and where.

But I was afraid
I couldn't catch up
for I can't hop fast
as you do—
of course I could walk
on top of the snow
for I was on snowshoes
too.

But in the deep woods
I could have been lost
so I really didn't
quite dare—
And besides
you hadn't invited me,
little white snowshoe
hare.

Estelle Delano Clifton

50

PETER, THE SNOWMAN

It would not seem like winter,
   Without a snowman tall;
I've worked on one all morning,
   With Ted and little Paul.
This is a jolly snowman,
   With such a friendly smile,
We'll ask you out to meet him,
   In just a little while.

His hat belongs to Daddy,
   His button eyes are blue,
His bright red scarf and mittens
   Were knit by Cousin Sue.
We're going to call him Peter,
   We'd like to have him stay,
But sometime when we're all at school,
   He's sure to slip away.

Winifred C. Marshall

CHILD IN SNOW

Zipping
over
long-range white
of snow,
a child
on sled,
red on red,
darts
past
aided by
slope and wind—
"Hello"
and
"Goodby"
echoing—
breaking
new ground
with each descent,
delighting
always
in the making.

Lillie D. Chaffin

SNOW SENTRY

See the snowman
   all in white—
   standing still
   and silent-like
   as soft snow
   settles light
   on this cool
   long frosty night.

Crystal flakes spin
   round and fall,
   covering him
   beyond recall.

Still he'll stand
   sentry tall,
   keeping night-watch
   over all.

Kate Monroe

LET'S GO COASTING

Let us go coasting
   On my brand-new sled.

It is new and shiny;
   And is painted red!

It is big and roomy;
   We can ride it double.

Two can get on it
   Without any trouble.

You can help me pull it;
   We can ride together.

Let us go coasting,
   For it's splendid weather!

Get your coat and mittens;
   All the world is white.

Let us go coasting
   While the snow is just right!

Nona Keen Duffy

JANUARY

Little January
   Tapped at my door today,
And said, "Put on your winter wraps,
   And come outdoors to play."

Little January
   Is always full of fun;
Today we coasted down the hill,
   Until the set of sun.

Little January
   Will stay a month with me
And we will have such jolly times—
   Just come along and see.

Winifred C. Marshall

WINTER FUN

It's snowing, it's snowing, winter winds are blowing.
I think I'll go outside and play—
This is such a lovely day.
I'll skate and sled and have such fun,
Come and join me, everyone.

Zipper up your snowsuit,
Put your earmuffs on your head,
Tie a scarf around your neck,
A bright one—maybe red!
Now to put your skates on,
Buckle them very tight,
And don't forget your mittens.
Oh, how the wind does bite!

Now off we go a-skating,
Strike out, every one,
Skate along, be happy, and
Sing this little song—
    Skating, skating, sliding along on the ice,
    Skating, skating, winter fun is so nice,
    Skating, skating, how the wind does blow,
    Skating, skating, fun in the ice and snow!

But now it's time to skate back home.
The wind is strong—we're tired and blown.
Before we run again and play,
We'll build a fire, and there we'll stay
To warm ourselves, then be on our way—

Now we'll all go sledding,
Down the hill we go,
Coasting is such jolly fun
In the ice and snow!

I'm coasting down the hill,
When whoops! I take a spill!
Then up I jump, brush off the snow,
Then down again I go. Whoops!
And now I'll stop to play in the snow,
Guess what I'm making, or do you know?

Catherine Y. Hoagey

SKI LIFT

You ride up on the ski lift
To the mountain's snowy spire.
You sway high over chasms
On a sort of creaking wire.

You huddle on the narrow seat,
Secretly agreeing
That possibly the ski lift
Is scarier than skiing.

Ethel Jacobson

SNOW

Where would you like to go in the snow?
Where would you like to go?

I'd like to go to a hilltop.
And slide and slide and never stop,
Where the ground is slippery, sloshy cold
And the wind is brave and blustery bold.
That's where I'd like to go.

Where would you like to go in the snow?
Where would you like to go?

I'd like to go out on a lawn
And roll a man at early dawn
From fragile, fluttery, frosty flakes,
Then give him carrots and coats and rakes.
That's where I'd like to go.

If only it would snow!

Lillie D. Chaffin

A WINTER GARDEN

I have a winter garden
Here on the window sill,
Where lovely flowers blossom,
Though days are dark and chill.

Each day I bring them water
And tend them with great care;
But it is worth the trouble
To have a garden there.

When fleecy, white snow blankets
Have covered other flowers,
I'll have my indoor garden
To cheer the winter hours.

Winifred C. Marshall

A SNOWBALL

Make your fingers a scooper
And scoop up snow.
Pack it,
Round it,
Pack it,
Round it,
Back your arm and throw!

Dorothy S. Anderson

SNOW

Snow blows
In bunches.
Snow sparkles
And crunches.

Snow is clean and cold.
Snow is crisp, and yet
When it warms a little,
Snow is wet.

Any winter day, I know,
Is pleasanter when there is snow.

Lillie D. Chaffin

53

MARTIN LUTHER KING, JR.

Martin Luther King was born a freeman.
His father was born a freeman.
His grandfather was born a freeman.
From slavery shall come forth freemen.

Martin Luther King was born into a comfortable family.
He did not know hunger or poverty.
Neither did his father before him.
Those who have shall remember those who have not.

Martin Luther King fought for the rights of his people.
He fought for equal rights for all people.
He fought for those not free.
He fought for the poor.
He fought for those who needed help.
But Martin Luther King was a man of peace.
The fighting man was, in truth, a man of peace.

Martin Luther King was a great dreamer.
He saw in his heart the world as he would like it to be.
"I have a dream that one day on the red hills of Georgia
Sons of former slaves and sons of former slaveholders
Will sit down together at the table of brotherhood.
I have a dream that my four children
Will one day live in a nation where
They will not be judged by the color of their skin
But by the content of their character."

His dreams were exciting
And people wanted to believe.
The world wanted to believe.
They gave him a prize—
The Nobel Peace Prize.

"I accept this award," he said,
"With an abiding faith in America
And an audacious faith
In the future of mankind."

Martin Luther King came home.
He came home to go on fighting for equal rights.
Fighting against poverty.
Fighting for a better world.
Yet he was still a man of peace.

How does a man of peace fight?
He uses words.
He uses deeds.
He uses actions.
He does not hurt.
He does not destroy.
He does not kill.

But not all people believed in Martin Luther King.
They do not believe in his dream of world peace.
They are afraid of his promise of freedom.
These people will have to learn.
For the dream of Martin Luther King *will* come true.
The dream he talked about when he said,
"When we allow freedom to ring—
When we let it ring from every city and hamlet,
From every state and every city,
We will be able to speed up that day when
All God's children, black men and white men,
Jews and Gentiles, Protestants and Catholics,
Will be able to join hands and sing . . .
'Free at last, Free at last,
Great God Almighty, We are free at last.'"

Gerda G. Lakritz

FRANKLIN'S KITE

When Franklin flew his famous kite
  And drew the lightning's fire,
Coaxing from thunderclouds the bright
  Sparks on his "pointed wire,"
I wonder if he visioned how
  Electricity
Would be the servant it is now
  Of domesticity!

Ben Franklin could not "plug it in"
  And get his coffee boiling;
Nor start the toaster with a grin,
  Then go back to his toiling;
Good Madame Franklin did not use
  The "current" for her cleaning;
Nor dreamed that "Monday Wash Day Blues"
  Ben's "find" would rob of meaning.

Wherefore, as we turn on the light
  Which sends the shadows fleeting
Or press a button when at night
  We feel it's time for eating,
Let's honor early scientist Ben—
  His kite amid the thunder—
Since, but for pioneering then,
  Would there be an age of wonder?

Clarence M. Lindsay

ROBERT E. LEE

Soul of the Old South, and her pride!
  Great leader of her sons,
Who fiercely fought and grimly died
  Amid the flaming guns
Of Gettysburg and red Shiloh!
  Thy countrymen today
The measure of thy greatness know,
  Thou deathless Man in Gray!

"Son of the Old Dominion!" True
  To her at any cost!
Choosing to lead the valiant few,
  Be their cause won or lost!
Thy soul still marches on! We see
  Against the fadeless past
Thy knightly figure, deathless Lee,
  Imperishably cast!

"Mars' Robert!" Chieftain of the host
  Which wore the Southern gray!
Today thou art a nation's boast;
  And shall be so, for aye!
The Stars and Bars are folded now,
  In glory, not in shame!
And a united people bow
  To Lee's immortal name!

Clarence M. Lindsay

MISTAKES

I like to hear what Franklin did
  When he was just a boy—
Spent all his birthday pennies for
  A little penny toy.

I like to know that great men, too,
  When they were young like me,
Sometimes made as bad mistakes
  As mine turn out to be.

They learned a lot from their mistakes
  And later on won fame.
Perhaps, if I try very hard,
  I can do the same.

Clara G. Cornell

GROUNDHOG DAY

If Candlemas Day be fair and bright
Winter will have another flight;
But if it be dark with clouds and rain,
Winter is gone, and will not come again.

Traditional Scottish Rhyme

FEBRUARY

Oh, you may sing of bonny May
   And April's silver showers,
The red of gay October's leaves,
   Or August's fragrant flowers;

But give me jolly, crackling fires
   And snowflakes, soft and merry,
The month of holidays and fun,
   Gay, friendly February!

Frances Gorman Risser

ST. VALENTINE

A dear old man,
As I've heard tell,
Had many friends
He loved very well.
  He walked with children,
  Up and down dell—
  He played with them,
  And stories would tell.
    Now when he was sick,
    This dear old man
    Couldn't play or visit,
    So he had a fine plan.
      Friendly letters he wrote,
      And sent by the birds,
      From his opened windows.
      (That's what I've heard.)
        And those kind letters—
        Messages of love—
        Were from Mr. Valentine,
        And his postmen were doves.

Mabel Walter

I LIKE YOU

Although I saw you
The day before yesterday,
And yesterday and today,
This much is true—

I want to see you tomorrow, too!

Masuhito (eighth century)

A VALENTINE

A valentine—and it is mine;
  It tells a secret, too.
See underneath its lacy frills—
  "I send my love to you."

Ada Clark

IF I WERE A VALENTINE

Wish I were a valentine, valentine, valentine,
　Wish I were a valentine, shiny and new.

If I were a valentine, valentine, valentine,
　I would be your valentine, loving and true.

If I were a valentine, valentine, valentine,
　If I were a valentine, what would I do?

I'd fly away, fly away, fly away, fly away,
　If I were a valentine, I'd fly to you.

Kathleen Eiland

THE ONLY ONE

Crimson hearts, and charming laces,
Pretty, smiling, dimpled faces,
Dainty bits of verse and rhymes,
Oh, what pretty valentines!

I must buy one for my mother.
Of fair ladies there's no other
That I love so much, you see;
She's the only girl for me.

Carolyn R. Freeman

VALENTINE FOR GRANNY

Dear Granny, here's a valentine;
　I made it just for you;
This rosebud and this paper lace
　Are fastened tight with glue.

This little heart I painted red,
　These flowers I made blue,
And Granny, look, here are the words,
　"Dear Granny, I love you."

Solveig Paulson Russell

OUR VALENTINE

I know the nicest valentine
You ever could discover,
With eyes of blue and curls of brown,
And dimples just all over.

This pretty little valentine
Was sent last year to Mother;
Today he is just one year old—
My little baby brother.

Alice Du Bois

MY VALENTINE

I made a valentine,
so different and new.
The heart isn't all red,
but red, white, and blue.

It's real patriotic
And real loving, too.
I almost forgot;
I made it for you!

Clare Miseles

JACK FROST'S VALENTINE

Wee Jack Frost made for his friends
  A charming valentine—
Dainty flowers of finest lace
  Of fairy-like design:
Laid the present on the window,
  Quickly ran away,
And thought that it would bring to us
  A message sweet and gay.

Mr. Sun said, "Well, just look!"
  And laughed full merrily;
Never seemed to understand
  'Twas left for you and me!
And, because he did not know
  That it was yours and mine,
He melted it to crystal dew
  And *drank* our valentine!

Sarah Grames Clark

VALENTINE!

I made a snowman yesterday
So jolly, fat, and fine;
I pinned a red heart on his chest
And named him "Valentine."

Last night a warm, sweet breeze blew by,
And stole his heart so gay;
My snowman melted on the spot
And quickly ran away!

Frances Gorman Risser

SNOWMAN'S VALENTINE

I have a jolly snowman,
  The best I've ever had.
I'm giving him a valentine
  That ought to make him glad.
For though he's very handsome
  And sound in every part,
I noticed only yesterday
  He hasn't any heart.
So quickly with my scissors
  And paper red and fine
I've made a fancy little heart:
  My snowman's valentine!

Leland B. Jacobs

A SPECIAL VALENTINE

"It's time to make my valentines,"
  To Mother I had said.
"I must have ribbons and I'll need
  Some slices of your bread."

"What will you make?" my mother asked;
  I did not tell her, though.
"You'll be surprised," was my reply,
  "But you'll be pleased, I know."

Out to the kitchen then I ran,
  And soon I'd finished there
My strange new kind of valentine
  That, none the less, was fair.

I hung my valentines outdoors
  All tied with ribbons red,
And snowflakes made a dainty lace
  For each white heart of bread.

When Mother saw what I had made,
  She smiled and said, "How fine!
Now all the hungry little birds
  Will have a valentine!"

Leland B. Jacobs

NOBODY LOVES ME

Somedays,
nobody loves me
so I go down the names
I know:
I hate Martha
I hate James
I hate Selma
I hate Jo.
Nobody likes me,
that I know.

Somedays,
everyone loves me
so I go down the names
I know:
I love Martha
I love James
I love Selma
I love Jo.
Everyone loves me,
I know so!

Charlotte Zolotow

DO YOU LOVE ME?

Do you love me
Or do you not?
You told me once
But I forgot.

Unknown

LOVE

Ricky was "L" but he's home with the flu,
Lizzie, our "O," had some homework to do,
Mitchell, "E," prob'ly got lost on the way,
So I'm all of love that could make it today.

Shel Silverstein

BE MY NON-VALENTINE

I have searched my Thesaurus through
to find a synonym for you;
here are some choice words that may do:

you're a hoddy-doddy, a dizzard, a ninny, a dolt,
a booby, a looby, a fribble, a gowk,
a nonny, a nizy, a nincompoop,
a churl, a scrimp, a knag, a trapes,
a lubber, a marplot, an oaf, a droil,
a mopus, a flat, a muff, a doit,
a mugwump, a dimwit, a flunkey, a swab,
a bane, a murrain, a malking, a pox,
a sloven, a slammerkin, a draggel tail,
frumpery, scrannel, and kickshaw, too!

Eve Merriam

ON LINCOLN'S BIRTHDAY

On Lincoln's birthday
  I try to walk
Straighter and taller,
  And try to talk

To the folks I meet
  In the kindly way
Lincoln would do
  If he lived today.

On Lincoln's birthday
  It seems I hear
These words on the wind,
  Steady and clear:

"Fourscore and seven
  Years ago . . ."
And around my heart
  Creeps a warm bright glow.

On Lincoln's birthday
  I sometimes plan
The person I'll be
  When I'm a man;

And the picture I dream
  That never grows dim
Is of myself
  Being much like him!

Elaine V. Emans

LINCOLN

Born in grinding poverty,
  Exposed to frontier strife,

Poor in things material,
  But, oh, how rich his life!

May we learn the lesson that
  This thought of Lincoln brings;

Life never can be measured well
  By its material things.

Alice Crowell Hoffman

60

THE YOUTHFUL LINCOLN

When Lincoln was a growing boy,
He had few books—not any toy;
He had no lovely shaded light
That he could read beneath at night.

And yet he had the will to learn,
And while the fire logs would burn,
Beside their blaze he often read,
Before he sought his humble bed.

And if perhaps we pause when we
Grow tired, and think of hardships he
Endured, and yet grew kind and strong,
We shall not be discouraged long.

Margaret E. Bruner

FEBRUARY THOUGHTS

When I've been reading stories
Of a long time ago,
I look around at all the friends
And playmates that I know.

I think, "Well, maybe Jim will be
A president some day;
And perhaps people years from now
Will read of Ann or Kay."

Each one of them might render
Some service fine and true;
For Washington and Lincoln
Once were children, too.

And if they grew to be great men
And shaped our country's ways,
We children who are growing now
May serve in future days.

So we who love our country
Should strive each day to be
Wise and worthy leaders
Of the land where men are free.

Solveig Paulson Russell

AS ONE LAD TO ANOTHER

I wish we'd been boys together,
    Abe Lincoln, I really do;
Somehow I cannot help thinking
    I'd have learned so much from you.

You studied under conditions
    That might well have made me quail;
In your quest for education
    You knew not a word like *fail*.

And you always made the utmost
    Of everything that you had;
You saw a lot of fun in life
    And you joked when you were sad.

You were ever true and earnest,
    And you saw so much of good
In folks whom others slighted—
    You sensed man's brotherhood.

Though life denies that I should be
    A boy, dear Abe, *with* you,
I still can try with all my might
    To be a boy *like* you.

Alice Crowell Hoffman

LINCOLN MONUMENT:
WASHINGTON

Let's go see old Abe
Sitting in the marble and the moonlight,
Sitting lonely in the marble and the moonlight,
Quiet for ten thousand centuries, old Abe.
Quiet for a million, million years.

Quiet—

And yet a voice forever
Against the
Timeless walls
Of time—
Old Abe.

Langston Hughes

LINCOLN SPOKE

He sat on a log at noontime.
He heard the sound of a bird.
His thoughts took form within him.
He spoke
And a forest heard.

He stood in the halls of justice
That the cause of right might be served.
He reasoned with homespun humor.
He spoke
And his neighbors heard.

From the pinnacle of high office,
Appearing uncouth and absurd,
He bitterly fought injustice.
He spoke
And a nation heard.

He rose on a field of battle
To say a few solemn words.
His great heart torn within him,
He spoke
And mankind heard.

Hazel M. Thomson

LITTLE ABE LINCOLN

Little Abe Lincoln,
    Tousled head bent low,
    Reading by the firelight's
    Red and fitful glow,
With charcoal for a pencil,
    A shovel for a slate,
At work and not complaining
Against an unkind fate!
    Little Abe Lincoln,
    Dreaming lofty dreams,
    Learning mighty secrets
    By the log fire's beams—
How to shape great dreams into
A living heart's desire,
Wise, untutored little lad,
A-sprawl before the fire!

Frances Gorman Risser

WASHINGTON

He played by the river when he was young,
He raced with rabbits along the hills,
He fished for minnows, and climbed and swung,
And hooted back at the whippoorwills.
Strong and slender and tall he grew—
And then, one morning, the bugles blew.

Over the hills the summons came,
Over the river's shining rim.
He said that the bugle called his name,
He knew that his country needed him,
And he answered, ''Coming!'' and marched away
For many a night and many a day.

Perhaps when the marches were hot and long
He'd think of the river flowing by
Or, camping under the winter sky,
Would hear the whippoorwill's far-off song.
Working or playing, in peace or strife,
He loved America all his life!

Nancy Byrd Turner

YOU CANNOT TELL

When Lincoln and George Washington
    Were little boys like me,
They never thought when they grew up
    That they would ever be

The President; and boys and girls
    Over books would pore
That told the way each worked and played
    So many years before.

Perhaps *I* should be careful,
    And live my boyhood well,
For sometime they might read of *me*—
    You really cannot tell!

Daisy Jenney Clay

A WISH FOR FEBRUARY

The Father of His Country
    Was once a lad like me.
He played and wrestled on the green
    And swung from leafy tree.
But when his country called him
    He put aside his play.
I hope that I, like Washington,
    May serve my land some day!

Donovan Marshall

OLD SONG

Americans, rejoice;
While songs imploy the voice,
    Let trumpets sound.
The thirteen stripes display
In flags and streamers gay,
'Tis Washington's birthday,
    Let joy abound.

Long may he live to see
This land of liberty
    Flourish in peace;
Long may he live to prove
A grateful people's love,
And late to heaven remove,
    Where joys ne'er cease.

Fill the glass to the brink,
Washington's health we'll drink,
    'Tis his birthday.
Glorious deeds he has done,
By him our cause is won,
Long live great Washington!
    Huzza! Huzza!

Anonymous

COLONIAL DAYS

A very young miss
    In George Washington's day
Would go out to ride
    With a horse and a sleigh.
She would wear a long cloak
    And a hood lined with down
And buckled shoes twinkling
    From under her gown.

          Kate Englehardt Clark

A NATION'S HERO

The flags fly, the bands play;
Give him the honor due
To one who served his country well,
A leader brave and true.
First in defense and first in peace;
In our hearts, as of yore,
He holds first place, George Washington,
Our hero, evermore.

          Winifred C. Marshall

GEORGE WASHINGTON

I wonder if George Washington
Was very fond of books,

And if he liked to hunt and fish,
And wade in little brooks.

I wonder if his pocket bulged
Like mine with precious things,

With marbles, cookies, tops, and balls,
And nails, and glass, and strings.

I wonder if he whistled tunes
While mending broken toys—

My father says George Washington
Was much like other boys.

          Winifred C. Marshall

HOW WASHINGTON DRESSED

When Washington was president,
    He wore the queerest clothes;
His shoes had silver buckles on—
    Now, why, do you suppose?

His suit was made of velvet cloth
    With buckles at the knee;
He wore lace ruffles on his coat
    When he went out to tea.

His hair was tied with ribbons, too,
    And braided like a girl's.
How could he be a president,
    And wear his hair in curls?

          Gertrude M. Robinson

VALLEY FORGE

Others may be forgetful,
    And little interest show,
But Valley Forge remembers
    A winter long ago.

When eyes sank deep with hunger,
    And the snow and the sleet.
Her ground still feels the pressure
    Of bare and bleeding feet.

Yea more. She still remembers
    The labor and the care
Of one who in her shadows
    Was often bowed in prayer.

Others may be forgetful,
    Now that the land is great,
But Valley Forge remembers
    It costs to make a state.

          Clarence Edwin Flynn

THOMAS ALVA EDISON

Thomas Alva Edison,
  A most unusual boy,
Never really bothered much
  With any childish toy.

His teacher thought he couldn't learn
  And sent him home from school,
But Tommy's mother knew for sure
  He wasn't any fool.

He worked as newsboy on a train,
  He learned to telegraph.
The way he concentrated
  Made some people laugh.

Thomas Alva Edison
  Had inventions by the score.
In his laboratory
  He kept inventing more.

The phonograph, electric light
  (With fuses, sockets, too),
A super storage battery,
  And movies, were a few.

If not for Mr. Edison
  How dull our lives would be!
We might not have the radio,
  The X-ray, or TV.

Vivian Gouled

THE WIZARD

Who was the Wizard of Menlo Park?
He conquered the dark.
He pierced the night
  with electric light
  captured in bubbles,
  glassy and tight!

Science or magic?
He even found
The way to capture the waves of sound
Upon a cylinder spinning round!
Machines to give us the tunes that swing—
The Wizard produced this wonderful thing!

Relaxing in play, he busied his brain,
Inventing his own electric train.
All his skeptical scientist friends
  zoomed up the hills
  and around the bends;
  then thanked their host
  for a wonderful lark—
Tom Edison, Wizard of Menlo Park!

Elsie S. Lindgren

EDISON

Little Alva Edison
Wanted to know why
White snow fell
From a slate-gray sky.

Why there was a rainbow,
Why there was a dawn,
Why there were dewdrops
On the summer's lawn.

His friends and relations
With many a sigh
Called Alva Edison
"Little Why, Why."

But he learned the answers.
And he banished the dark.
Then they called him
The Wizard of Menlo Park.

Jean Brabham McKinney

Spring

Signal the end of the long winter days with these lilting spring poems. From March winds to May flowers, there's one for every mood. Look here for those hard-to-find poems about St. Patrick's Day, Easter, Mother's Day, Memorial Day.

GOOD-BY AND HELLO!

Good-by, ice skates.
Good-by, sled.
Good-by, winter.
Spring's ahead!

Good-by, leggings.
Good-by, snow.
Good-by, winter.
Spring, hello!

Hello, crocus.
Hello, kite.
Good-by, winter.
Spring's in sight!

Hello, jump rope.
Hello, swing.
Good-by, winter!
Hello, spring!

Barbara Anthony

SPRING'S SIGNS

Forsythia, tulips
Are some of Spring's signs—
And they're painting the streets
With fresh yellow lines!

Lee Avery Reed

THIS MONTH

This month is no secret. It isn't July
When days are long and the sun is high.
It isn't December when snow lies deep
And none of the flowers have awakened from sleep.
It isn't September when bright leaves fall,
Or even October when corn's grown tall.

It's a month that's a rogue, and seldom mild,
That often behaves like a naughty child;
It grabs off hats and blows trash high
And sends clouds scudding across the sky.
It snatches at coats and streams dogs' hair
And whistles and screeches everywhere.
It spins windmills and makes kites sail.
And forces branches to bend and flail.

It's a blustery, flustery set of days
With a promise of spring and better ways.
It's an active month, and one we need.
You say it's March? Yes, indeed!

Solveig Paulson Russell

MARCH

Oh, March is a blustering
  Ruddy-faced boy,
Who blows out his cheeks
  And whistles for joy,
Who stamps through mud puddles
  And wades through slush,
Who never plays gently
  But always must rush.

He's a stout, sturdy fellow,
  Brimful of fun,
Who chases old Winter
  And makes him run.
Oh, he's rough and he's tough,
  But he has a kind heart,
And he's always on hand
  To help the Spring start.

Solveig Paulson Russell

MARCH

You're loud,
You're noisy,
  A blustery old chap!
You whistle,
You moan,
  You tear at my cap!

You blow,
You scowl,
  But, March, you are fair!
Part lion,
Part lamb,
  Now spring's in the air!

Mildred Pittinger

THE MERRY MONTH OF MARCH

The cock is crowing,
The stream is flowing,
The small birds twitter,
The lake doth glitter,
The green field sleeps in the sun;
  The oldest and youngest
  Are at work with the strongest;
The cattle are grazing,
Their heads never raising;
There are forty feeding like one!

Like an army defeated
The snow hath retreated,
And now doth fare ill
On the top of the bare hill;
The plough-boy is whooping anon, anon.
  There's joy in the mountains;
  There's life in the fountains;
Small clouds are sailing,
Blue sky prevailing;
The rain is over and gone!

William Wordsworth

MARCH

A blue day,
a blue jay
and a good beginning.
One crow,
melting snow—
spring's winning!

Elizabeth Coatsworth

SPRING'S MAGIC

March is:
  mud,
  mops,
  measles,
  cough drops,
  snow,
  sleet,
  sniffles,
  wet feet,
  soggy woolens,
  leaden skies,
  no glad sights
  for tired eyes.
Then! Everything
comes into focus
With a crocus.

Faye Tanner Cool

SPRING IS COMING

March has warmed the icy blasts,
And the wintertime is past.

Now we hear the robins sing—
Happy harbingers of spring.

Little buds will wake from sleep,
From the ground their faces peep.

Do you know why all is fun?
Spring is coming on the run.

Dorothy Hevener

THE SUGAR CALL

Now flickers call, and robins call,
  And bluebirds in the wood,
"Oh, hurry, hurry, hurry!
  Here's sugar that is good.
Oh, hurry, hurry, hurry!
  Bring buckets, spouts, and spoon,
The maple sap is running free
  In March's sunny noons.
Hepaticas are peeping through
  The dead leaves in the wood.
Oh, hurry, hurry, hurry!
  Sugaring time is good.
Oh, hurry, hurry, hurry!
  The snow is melting fast.
The time to gather sugar
  Will soon be quickly past."

Norman C. Schlichter

A MARCH SURPRISE

The trees are still asleep today
  And do not seem to know
A storm came by last night and heaped
  Their branches full of snow.

See how they start up with surprise
  As one by one they wake.
"Why, gracious me!" they seem to say,
  And give themselves a shake.

Ralph Marcellino

WHO'D FORGET?

When March is going, going
  To robins' gay farewell,
And April, blossom-laden,
  Is close to hill and dell;

When March is going, going,
  Oh, none would have her stay,
But who'd forget to thank her
  For preparing April's way?

Norman C. Schlichter

KITE SONG

All the other seasons
  Added up together
Never can compare
  With kite-flying weather!

Like a bird skimming
  Across the blue sky,
My kite travels swiftly—
  Beautiful and high!

The cord often runs
  Stinging through my hand,
As my bird soars higher,
  Higher o'er the land!

But all too soon twilight
  Lowers on the town,
And I must haul my bird
  Down, down, down!

Elaine V. Emans

A KITE

I often sit and wish that I
Could be a kite up in the sky,
And ride upon the breeze and go
Whichever way I chanced to blow.

Anonymous

MARCH WIND

We made a brand-new kite today,
And soon as we were through
We came out here to fly it,
And the wind just blew and blew.
And now the kite's a tiny speck;
We've used up all the string;
I'd like to go and get some more.
Anne's such a tiny thing
To hold the kite all by herself;
I wouldn't let her try,
For fear I might look back and see
Anne sailing through the sky.

Eleanor Dennis

OPEN THE DOOR

"Open the door!"
It's March that's knocking there so gay.
"Open the door!"
I've heard his merry, boisterous knock before;
Just hear him shouting, "Hurry, come and play,
And bring your kite, for it's a windy day!
Open the door!"

Evantha Caldwell

THE WIND

I saw you toss the kites on high
And blow the birds about the sky;
And all around I heard you pass,
Like ladies' skirts across the grass—
  O wind, a-blowing all day long,
  O wind, that sings so loud a song!

I saw the different things you did,
But always you yourself you hid.
I felt you push, I heard you call,
I could not see yourself at all—
  O wind, a-blowing all day long,
  O wind, that sings so loud a song!

O you that are so strong and cold,
O blower, are you young or old?
Are you a beast of field and tree,
Or just a stronger child than me?
  O wind, a-blowing all day long,
  O wind, that sings so loud a song!

Robert Louis Stevenson

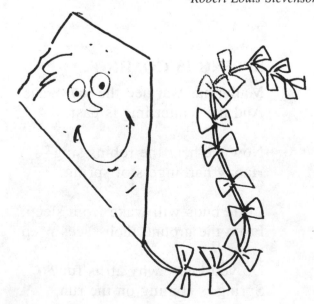

NEVER MIND, MARCH

Never mind, March, we know
When you blow
You're not really mad
Or angry or bad;
You're only blowing the winter away
To get the world ready for April and May.

Unknown

MERRY MARCH

Merry, mad March comes in with a bound,
Tossing our caps and our kites all around,
Whisking the cobwebs out of the sky,
Teasing wee birdies just learning to fly,
Giving each tree-child a vigorous shake,
Telling each bud it is time to awake,
Jerking leaf-coverlets off sleepy heads,
Routing young flowerets from earthy beds,
Then with a song that makes work only play,
Merry, mad March goes dancing away.

Nancy Fritz Moon

WINDY WORD

I am the Wind
And you'd better watch out!
I can run, I can fly;
I can whistle and shout.

I can tap on your window
And howl at your door,
Tug on your coat tails,
Bellow and roar.

But in March I'm the loudest;
Look out for my might!
For when you're not looking
I'll steal your new kite.

Jean Conder Soule

MARCH

A boy with a kite
In windy weather
Tying the earth
And sky together.

May Richstone

OLD MAN MARCH WIND

That Old Man March Wind blusters through the town,
Twisting the tree tops, blowing chimneys down,
Rattling the windows, shaking the doors,
Rushing around corners with howls and roars.

That Old Man March Wind will chase you down the street,
And if you're not careful, he'll blow you off your feet.
He'll set your hat spinning and snatch at your cloak,
And scatter your belongings, and think it all a joke.

Says Old Man March Wind, "I'm cleaning house for spring—
Sweeping up the rubbish, dusting everything,
Fanning the air, polishing the sky—"
Says Old Man March Wind, "I'm blowing winter by!"

Julia Powell

ST. PATRICK'S GREEN

Oh, I love to see the shamrocks
    Boys wear March seventeen,
And I love the girls' green ribbons,
    And bits of evergreen;
For they stand for brave St. Patrick,
    So fearless and so good—
Oh! the Irish ought to love him,
    Just as everybody should!

Bertha E. Bush

ST. PATRICK'S DAY

Oh, don't forget that blustery March
    Brings in St. Patrick's Day,
When all of Ireland's children
    Sing a blithe and gladsome lay,
And, scattered all about the world,
    The color emerald green
In honor of St. Patrick
    On the seventeenth is seen.

Sarah Grames Clark

BUD O'MALLY

Bud O'Mally, with his very red hair,
    And his very, very, very green tie,
Sure! he was a pleasing sight
    For good St. Patrick's eye;

Sweet Miss Tulip thought him
    A new posy, without doubt;
And all agreed who saw him
    That Bud had blossomed out.

Carolyn Shaw Rice

ERIN'S ISLE

There's a charmin' bit o' country
    That is known as Erin's Isle,
Where merry winds make music
    And the fairies dance the while.

'Tis the land of the shillalah,
    Of the shamrock and hilleen,
And boys and girls show loyalty
    A-wearing of the green.

Sure, "The Wearing of the Green" is sung,
    Wherever there is found
A loyal son of Erin's Isle
    The whole wide world around;

So, although 'tis not our country,
    We'll join with theirs our lay,
And sing "The Wearing of the Green"
    On good St. Patrick's Day.

Beulah Sisson

HAPPY APRIL FOOL'S DAY VERBS

I saw a cowslip through the fence,
A horsefly in the store,
I saw a boardwalk up the street,
A stone step by a door.
I saw a mill race up the road,
A daybreak through the gloom.
I saw a nightfall on my lawn,
A clock run in the room.
I saw a peanut stand up high,
A sardine box in town,
A bedspring at the garden gate,
An inkstand on the ground.
You don't believe all this, do you?
For not a single thing is true.
It's just a silly way to say,
"Happy April Fool's Day!"

Dorothy D. Warner

MISS JONES

Pretty Miss Jones enjoys valentines
  Exactly as much as we children do,
But she doesn't care about Fourth of July
  Except that it happens when school is through.

She's not so excited about Halloween
  As she is about Christmas or Easter vacation,
Or Washington's birthday, or Abraham Lincoln's.
  Those noblest heros of our great nation.

But Miss Jones tells us the day she likes best
  Is a day when we still have to go to school;
She even reminded the class it's tomorrow,
  When we can be bad and say April Fool!

We had planned to put a few frogs in her desk,
  But now we don't know what to do or believe
When she tells us, and giggles, we'd better behave—
  As if she had something worse up her sleeve!

Harry Behn

APRIL FOOL

A snowfall came on April first,
  After the buds were out.
The pussy willows shook their heads.
  It made the crocus pout.

The bluebirds hopped from branch to branch,
  But never stopped their song;
They knew the snow was just a joke,
  And couldn't stay there long!

Inez George Gridley

APRIL FOOL!

This spring
The birds won't sing,
The flowers won't bud,
There'll be no rain or mud,
Grass won't turn green,
Toads won't be seen,
Ice won't melt on stream or pool—
APRIL FOOL!

Carolyn Sue Peterson

FIRST DAY OF APRIL

On the first day of April
if someone should say,
  "I'll give you a monster,
  a basket of hay,
  a ride in a rocket,
  and ten games to play,"
just laugh and remember . . .
It's APRIL FOOL'S DAY!

Vivian Gouled

APRIL

So here we are in April, in showy, blowy April,
    In frowsy, blowsy April, the rowdy, dowdy time
In soppy, sloppy April, in wheezy, breezy April,
    In ringing, stinging April, with a singing swinging rhyme.

The smiling sun of April on the violets is focal,
    The sudden showers of April seek the dandelions out;
The tender airs of April make the local yokel vocal,
    And he raises rustic ditties with a most melodious shout.

So here we are in April, in tipsy gypsy April,
    In showery, flowery April, the twinkly, sprinkly days;
In tingly, jingly April, in highly wily April,
    In mighty, flighty April with its highty-tighty ways!

The duck is fond of April, and the clucking chickabiddy
    And other barnyard creatures have a try at caroling;
There's something in the air to turn a stiddy kiddy giddy,
    And even I am forced to raise my croaking voice and sing.

Ted Robinson

CHANDELIER

Crystal prisms in the sky
Smile their twinkling light.
Truly the stars have gift-wrapped
This lovely April night!

Roberta Lindsay Peeden

APRIL SNOW

Snow slipped quietly down last night
When the world was fast asleep.
This morning jonquils and hyacinths
Waked up and tried to peep
Over the feathery blanket of white
That covered all the ground.
Branches, bending beneath its weight,
Complained with creaking sounds.
North Wind blew a blustering blast.
''I'll chase the snow,'' he said.
But he couldn't and finally,
Warm Mr. Sun smiled it away instead.

Jean Horton Berg

PAUL REVERE

The silversmith saw,
One April night
Two lanterns shine
From the church's height.

He jumped on his horse;
Its silver-shod feet
On the ribbonlike road
Were sure and fleet.

The moonlight was dripping
Like silver down
On each sleeping household
And silent town.

And the silversmith's voice
Rang clarion clear
As he called, ''Wake up all!
The British are near.''

Jean Brabham McKinney

APRIL LACE

It all began in such innocence;
More like a mirage than reality.
One had not expected
Any particular change,
Nothing had been arranged.
And yet, upon closer observation
And with certain confirmation,
Frozen particles of whiteness
Had fluffed itself into
Flakes
Of
Snow.

Susan Soward

A WELCOME MONTH IS APRIL

Said a tiny white cloud in the blue, blue sky,
  "I'm here because it's April!"
And one golden ray of the sun replied,
  "I always shine in April!"
Then came a great storm cloud, with heavy gray sack,
And said, "Little sunbeam and cloud, you come back!"
He packed them away and I heard him say,
  "It always *rains* in April!"

Said a tiny green brook as it laughed along,
  "I'll sing to welcome April,"
And the bluebird returning soon heard the song
  And said, "I'll trill for April."
Then that rascal Jack Frost, with his merriest laugh,
Sent snowflakes a-flying all over the path!
Said the bird to the brook, "Will you please look—
  There's *snow* again, in April!"

Said a wee little girl with golden hair
  "I need spring clothes in April!"
But the chill of the wind made her aunt declare,
  "It's always *cold* in April!"
Then, will you believe it, that very same day
The round sun invited the south wind to play—
The air was as warm as a day in May,
  Though it was only April!

I think you'll agree with me when I say,
  "A question mark is April."
The clouds and the sun and the south winds play
  Their merry tricks in April!
So, when it is sunny look out for a shower,
And though it is shining, 'twill rain in an hour—
Whatever the weather we say together,
  "A welcome month is April!"

Sarah Grames Clark

APRIL SHOWERS

April skies are weeping
  Tears of silver rain
On the buds still sleeping
  In the verdant lane.

Now the clouds which lower
  Clear in dazzling light,
And the sudden shower
  Yields to sunbeams bright!

April's merely chaffing!
  First, the raindrops cool;
Then the bright skies laughing—
  Playing April Fool!

Clarence M. Lindsay

APRIL FLOWERS

Sing a song of April flowers,
Colors bright in all.
Crocus buds inside the gate,
Tulips by the wall,

Daffodils and lilies fair
In the garden green,
These with other April flowers
Make a pleasant scene.

Colors yellow, pink, and blue
Mingle with the red.
Rainbow colors everywhere
'Round the violet bed.

Sing a song of April flowers,
Colors bright and gay,
Making peaceful Easter scenes
For the holiday.

Dorothy Hevener

INTERLUDE

A-clitter, a-clatter! I wonder what's the matter?
Why this splashing and this dashing against my window pane?

It's just the merry ditty, so musical and pretty,
The tapping, rapping spring song of the merry April rain.

A-pitter, a-patter! Now something is the matter.
What's the glimmer and the glitter on the still wet pane?

Oh, it's just a sunbeam smiling, so bewitching, so beguiling—
A brilliant interlude between the spring songs of the rain.

M. Lucille Ford

THE FRIENDLY SHOWER

We like a friendly little shower
Which lasts quite often half an hour—
  The flowers and I—

It flies across the hillside fast,
And finds our pleasant garden last,
  Then hurries by.

We like a little friendly shower,
And never mind the dark clouds that lower—
  The flowers and I—

For soon the golden sun peeps out,
The fountain leaps with joyous shout,
  Blue smiles the sky.

Alice Thorn Frost

APRIL RAIN DANCE

Pitter! Patter! drops of rain
Dancing on the windowpane!
Sometimes fast and sometimes slow
Up and down the glass they go,
Making their own music sweet
With the patter of their feet—
April!
    April!
        April!

Pitter! Patter! tinkling sound
As they madly whirl around;
Pit-ter! Pat-ter! sudden change
To a tempo low and strange.
See the rainbow jewels shine
On crystal slippers beating time—
April!
    April!
        April!

Marion Doyle

MOTHER GOOSE

Rain, rain, go away,
Come again some other day.

Rain, rain, go to Spain,
Never show your face again.

I LIKE IT WHEN IT'S MIZZLY

I like it when it's mizzly
and just a little drizzly
so everything looks far away
and make-believe and frizzly.

I like it when it's foggy
and sounding very froggy.
I even like it when it rains
on streets and weepy windowpanes
and catkins in the poplar tree
and *me*.

Aileen Fisher

SPRING RAIN SONG

Cheerily the silver rain
    Knocks upon the windowpane.
Patter! Patter! Hear the sound!
On the roofs and on the ground.
Beating out a quick refrain,
    Hear the music of the rain.

Gentle spring has come at last;
    Winter now is overpast.
Drenched are forest, field, and glen;
Brought to life is earth again.
Beating out a gay refrain,
    Hear the music of the rain!

Little children love the rain,
    As it splashes on the pane;
Watch the streams that swiftly pour
Sidewalks and the roadside o'er.
Cry they, "Welcome, rain of spring,
    For the treasures that you bring."

May D. Dryant

WHERE

Where is the rain that fell last week?
Playing tag in a mountain creek;
Feeding the roots of a blossoming tree;
Visiting friends back home in the sea;
Waking a seed lying withered and dry;
Boarding an airliner back to the sky.

Where is the wind that blew last night?
Joining a jet-stream altitude flight;
Teaching an eaglet to wheel and soar;
Cleaning a littered, trampled shore;
Singing through rocks to a far-off peak;
Ferrying raindrops that fell last week.

Helen T. Widoe

APRIL RAIN SONG

Let the rain kiss you.
Let the rain beat upon your head with silver liquid drops.
Let the rain sing you a lullaby.

The rain makes still pools on the sidewalk.
The rain makes running pools in the gutter.
The rain plays a little sleep-song on our roof at night—

And I love the rain.

Langston Hughes

LOVE AFFAIR

In the aftermath
Of a rainy day
As I skirted puddles
Along the way,
A blur of branch
Leaned down to me
And I got kissed
By a maple tree.

May Richstone

WHO LIKES THE WIND?

"I," said the kite,
"I like the wind,
I call it fun
To travel high and wink at the sun!"

"I," said the boat,
"I like the wind,
Just let it blow
And fill my sails and away I'll go!"

"I," said the thistle,
"I like the wind,
I call it fun
To leap and jump and before the wind run!"

Leah Gibbs Knobbe

MY PLAYMATE

I have an outdoor playmate
    Who's as jolly as can be;
Sometimes I'm sure he's hiding
    Up in our apple tree,
For the green leaves nod and rustle
    And seem to wave at me.

In springtime when we're playing,
    He is so very spry;
He catches up my paper kite
    And carries it up high
Above the tops of houses
    With their chimneys in the sky.

He often blows and whistles
    For me to come outside,
Then when I'm on my scooter
    He pushes while I ride—
And yet I've never seen him
    Though I've tried and tried and tried.

Mabel Niedermeyer

A PARTY GUEST

I had a birthday party
    And a spring breeze came.
It hadn't been invited, but
    It joined us just the same.

It slipped in at the window
    Just in time to take
Part in blowing out
    The candles on my cake.

Lucretia Penny

WIND SONG

I sit by the window
and watch the breeze
tingle the leaves
on all the trees.

I sit by the window
and hear the wind sing,
carrying spring,
making air ring.

Wind! Wind! Blow me a song.
Toss me a ship from the sea.
Fling me a willow tree tall and strong.
Whirl the world closer to me.

Mimi Brodsky

ARBOR DAY

"Tree Planting Day" they called it
In Nebraska long ago.
Now we call it Arbor Day, and
Oh, I love it so!
I love to plant a growing thing—
A tree, a shrub, a vine—
And know it will for years and years
Keep growing there, a sign
To children who come after me
That someone thought of them,
And left behind a living friend
More precious than a gem.

Betty Foust Smith

ARBOR DAY

I cannot dig a great big hole
   And set a tree into it,
But I can make a little hole
   And I am going to do it.

Then in the little hole I'll drop
   This acorn brown and shiny,
And that way I can plant a tree
   Although I am so tiny.

Alice Crowell Hoffman

ARBOR DAY

The seeds we plant today
With sun and rain and rest
Will grow to be the shade
That all the land wears best.

Dick Hayman

IN THE SHADE OF A TREE

I like to lie beneath a tree
and think of what trees mean to me
and everyone; their many uses.

They're used for houses and cabooses.
They make the fires so we cook
when we are camped beside a brook.
The campfires make us warm and dry
and send up sparks toward the sky.
They're used for boats for work or larks.
They're used for rafts, canoes, and arks.
They give us whistles from the willows
and even leaves that make soft pillows.
We sharpen their boughs into picks
and use them for our wiener sticks.
They're fun to climb; swing from their branches.

Trees in a row protect the ranches.
They harbor birds the whole year long,
who pay their rent with joyful song.
Trees give us many kinds of fruits.
In Holland, kids wear wooden boots.
Trees furnish flavoring and spice
and nuts and other things as nice.
In Portugal, the cork trees grow.
Trees give us rubber, too, you know.
That trees are useful, there's no doubt.
Are there some uses I left out?

Thelma Ireland

ONE MORE TIME

I can't believe. I don't believe.
I simply, simply won't believe
A rabbit comes at Easter time
To bring us eggs—

But then,

I do believe that you believe,
And there are others who believe,
And so perhaps for one more time,
I'll make believe again.

Margaret Hillert

AN EASTER PUZZLE

This morning, what do you suppose
    I found beside my door?
A nest of colored Easter eggs—
    Five or six or more.

I asked my own pet bunny,
    Who seems to love me so,
To tell me where they came from;
    I thought perhaps he'd know.

Yet not a single word he said,
    Though twice he blinked his eyes;
But I believe he really knows
    Because he looked so wise.

Alice Du Bois

EASTER EGGS

Sing a song of Easter eggs—
    Betsy counted eight,
Hidden in a grassy nook,
    By the garden gate;

Two beneath the lilac bush,
    Near the pansy bed;
Bob gave her a purple one;
    She gave Bob a red;

Four beneath a wild rosebush,
    Growing in the yard.
Let's help Betty count her eggs;
    It will not be hard.

Winifred C. Marshall

THE EASTER EGG HUNT

Early Easter morning,
With Dorothy and Don,
I went hunting Easter eggs
Upon the grassy lawn.

We searched in nooks and corners,
And in the rose bed, too,
And soon had filled our baskets
With red and green and blue.

I showed mine to my speckled hen,
And do you know, my dear,
She seemed to like her plain eggs best
And think that mine were queer.

Winifred C. Marshall

YOU MUST RUSH

You must rush to see a show,
And worry that you may be late,
And step on feet to find your seat,
Because those actors will not wait.

It's fun to see things on TV,
But you must get there on the minute,
'Cause on the dot they start the plot;
They won't wait to begin it.

But with a book you take a look,
And if there's something you must do,
Eat jam and bread, or go to bed,
The book will always wait for you.

Gina Bell-Zano

RAINY DAY

I used to hate a rainy day.
There were no outside games to play,
And even though our house was roomy
The gray rain made the inside gloomy.
Now, I don't mind the rain at all,
For when no friends come to call,
I've all the company I need.
I pick me out a book, and read!

Gina Bell-Zano

WHAT IS A BOOK?

A book is pages, pictures, and words;
A book is animals, people, and birds;
A book is stories of queens and kings,
Poems, and songs—so many things!
Curled in a corner where I can hide,
With a book I can journey far and wide.
Though it's only paper from end to end,
A book is a very special friend.

Lora Dunetz

LIBRARY

Books on tables,
Books on shelves.
Boys and girls,
Help yourselves.

Butterflies,
Lullabies,
Dolls that talk,
Fun with chalk,

Things to make,
Trips to take,
Winnie the Pooh,
Bambi too.

Treat them kindly—
Lovingly—
The wonderful books
At the library.

Thelma Kalbfleisch

THE LIBRARY

I'm a library;
Behind my door
Are shelves of books
From ceiling to floor.

Books that will take you
To far away lands,
To the Arctic snow,
To the desert sands.

Books that will shoot you
To Mars or a star—
Back thousands of years
Or beyond where you are.

So open the door
That will lead you to me—
To the library where
Adventure is free.

Jean Brabham McKinney

THE COMING OF MAY

May opened up her basket,
And I looked in to see
A sky of blue,
The great sun too,
Both smiling out at me.

May opened up her basket,
And out the flowers fell.
Their fragrance spilled
Until it filled
All nature with its spell.

May opened up her basket,
Her choristers were there!
Their welcoming
To joy and spring
Was wafted on the air.

She opened up her basket—
The world was blithely gay.
Earth knew again
The ample reign
And blessing of the May!

Leland B. Jacobs

MAY IS . . .

A blue sky shot with sunbeams,
Green shadows 'neath the trees,
The caroling of many birds,
A gentle, soft, warm breeze.

The fruit trees all in blossom,
Pale pink and pearly white,
The lilacs waving purple plumes,
A truly gorgeous sight.

Each flowering shrub a beautiful
Gigantic sweet bouquet,
In the month of birds and flowers,
Fragrant, lovely, merry May.

Maude M. Grant

THE NEW BONNET

I have a new bonnet
A pretty new bonnet,
A new yellow bonnet
To wear on May Day.

There are daffodils on it,
And flutes and frills on it.
On May Day I'll don it;
Oh, hurray for May!

Julia Powell

MAYTIME

Springtime came a-Maying
Over meadow, valley, hill,
In the early dawning
When all the earth was still.

Here she dropped a tulip,
There a lily fair,
And daffodils have fallen
From her flower-wreathed hair.

Over by the hedgerow
She dropped some violets down.
She left her posy tokens
At every door in town.

M. Lucille Ford

MAY DAY

It is May Day, birds are singing,
Winds from fairyland are playing,
Blossom-laden boughs are swaying!
Jonquils wave their golden banners,
Tulips light each crimson candle;
All the world's a bright May basket
With a rainbow for a handle.

Frances Gorman Risser

80

EXERCISES

Stand tall and stretch,
  reach up, up high;
  pretend you're a tree
  growing right through the sky.

Bend to the floor
  with your knees held straight;
  touch your heels 'til you look
  like the figure eight.

Spread out your arms
  from your waist, turn half round;
  back and forth like a clock
  that is being wound.

Hop, hop on one foot;
  then hop on the other;
  pretend you're a bird
  bobbing after its mother.

Leap up so high
  you could jump in a nest
  then flop down, cross-legged,
  and take your rest.

Bette Killion

MAY

May always brings the sunshine,
  May baskets, Mother's Day;
We always crown a May queen
  Upon the first of May.

The wild flowers spread a carpet;
  The larks and thrushes sing,
Broadcasting from the tree tops
  Sweet lyrics of the spring.

Around the stately Maypole,
  We weave the ribbons gay;
There's something very lovely
  About the month of May.

Winifred C. Marshall

HEALTH DAY

May Day is Health Day
  For children everywhere,
The day to think of healthy things
  Like food and sun and air;

The day to stop to value
  The blessing of good health,
And count it first in measuring
  The things that make for wealth.

A nation's biggest asset
  Is not concerned with gold,
But healthy minds and bodies
  In children, young and old.

So, each who loves his country
  Can strive to do his part
By trying to keep healthy
  In body, mind, and heart.

Solveig Paulson Russell

THE MAYPOLE

Winding round the Maypole,
  On a sunny day,
In and out the ribbons
  Weave a pattern gay.

Betty, Bob, and Teddy,
  Jean, and little Sue
Dance around the Maypole,
  With Jimmy, Don, and Prue.

In and out the ribbons
  Weave a pattern gay,
Winding round the Maypole,
  On the first of May.

Winifred C. Marshall

GUEST TIME

When we're expecting company
   Mother sets our house in shape;
No particle of dust and dirt
   Her brush and broom escape.

And Mother Nature does, you see,
   The very selfsame thing;
She makes March sweep her house quite clean
   For her house guest, Miss Spring.

Alice Crowell Hoffman

IT'S SPRING

Good-by, snow! Good-by, ice!
Though of course you're very nice,
I am glad you've gone away
Leaving us this fine spring day.

Here's my good old bat and ball!
Marbles, too! How are you all?
I am sure that I can play
With you now, 'most any day.

Good-by, winter! Though it's true
I've had lots of fun with you,
Now I just could shout and sing;
I'm so glad because it's spring!

Winnifred J. Mott

SIGNS OF SPRING

Tops are whirling,
Kites are swirling
   In the windy sky;

Hoops are rolling,
Children strolling;
   Surely spring is nigh.

Brooks are flowing,
Grasses growing,
   Birds are nesting, too;

Buds are breaking,
Flowers awak'ning;
   Spring's come back to you!

Mabel Niedermeyer

THE CALL OF SPRING

When spring begins
   Again to light
Our happy world
   With colors bright,

The robins all come
   Back to see
How beautiful
   The earth will be,

With crocus gold,
   And daffodils
Lighting meadows,
   Fields, and hills;

With leaves of green
   And tulips gay,
And birds arriving
   Every day.

Norman C. Schlichter

SPRING

First day of spring;
On the ancient plum tree
three open blossoms.

Lorraine Ellis Harr

SPRING CLEANING

In early spring the sky's gray rooms
Are cleaned and swept by windy brooms.
Housekeepers flick the dust about,
Then roll the bright blue carpet out.

Before the yearly task is done
And clouds are bleaching in the sun,
Someone up there shakes a mop
And snowflakes tumble down on top

Of fields and meadows, lakes and hills.
And where the winter cloud dust spills
Upon a robin in his tree,
He hides his head and can't agree
(Although perhaps he ought to try)
With all that cleaning in the sky!

Jean Conder Soule

SPRING ZING

rustling . . .
  rippling . . .
    flutter,
      flap;
bubbling . . .
  billowing . . .
    crackle,
      crack;
stirring . . .
  whirring . . .
    slither,
      snap;
blowing . . .
  flowing . . .
    tinkle,
      tap;
rolling . . .
  tolling . . .
    rip,
      rap;
singing . . .
  ringing . . .
    zip,
      zap.

Minnie Mondschein

GREEN-APPLE MORNING

It's a green-apple morning,
Polished with sun,
And here in the orchard
Mist is spun.
The sun's red crayon
Paints the hill
While orchard trees stand
Picture-still.
I run to the edge of
This new day,
And the green-apple morning
Slips away.

Mary Graham Bond

SPRING SONG

The violets are blooming
On hillside and in lane,
The meadow larks are broadcasting
That spring has come again.

The merry little brooklets
All run along and sing
This happy little theme song,
"It's spring! It's spring! It's spring!"

Winifred C. Marshall

BECAUSE IT'S SPRING

My father spades the garden,
　My mother rakes the yard;
My brother sails his newest kite,
　'Cause the South Wind blows so hard.

The snow is melting, melting,
　Where once it piled so high,
And yesterday, for dinner,
　We had fresh rhubarb pie.

The robin chirps and twists his head,
　He doesn't really sing;
And yesterday I saw the flash
　Of a red-bird's lovely wing.

The big white clouds go tumbling,
　Up where it's blue and high;
The tree tops are laughing, shrieking,
　As the wind goes sailing by.

I run and shout and scamper,
　I jump and laugh and sing;
I feel so wild and happy,
　Because, you know, it's spring.

Alice Curtis

SPRING SONG

The year's at the spring
And day's at the morn;
Morning's at seven;
The hillside's dew-pearled;
The lark's on the wing;
The snail's on the thorn;
God's in his heaven—
All's right with the world!

Robert Browning

WHEN SPRING CAME

When Spring came,
Leaves grew with a green fresh feeling,
And the warmth of the sun
Was beginning to be felt,
And the Animals of the Earth
Awoke, breathing the fresh new smell
Of life all over again.

It's like the wind,
Gently blowing,
Making love to everything
Before it moves on
Yet returning.

Tlingit Indian Song

SPRING IN ME

The sun is warm, the wind is soft,
　And in our apple tree,
A little bluebird sings a happy
　Springtime song to me.

On the lawn, where snow lay deep
　Not many weeks ago,
A hundred bright and sun yellow
　Dandelions grow.

The breeze blows little powdery clouds
　Across a sky of blue
I feel like singing little tunes
　For spring is in me, too.

Marian Kennedy

A SPRING MORNING

It's easy to wake up in spring—
　Oh, yes, it's really so—
To dress, then very quickly
　Down to my breakfast go.

For why should I stay in bed?
　A foolish thing to do!
When all the flowers are wide awake,
　I have to wake up, too.

Alix Thorn

HELICOPTER OVER WILDCAT MOUNTAIN

Where tongues of flame devoured the chaparral,
One blackened tree trunk, stark in silhouette,
Points to this motored bird whose flight lets fall
A shower of rye grass seed on Mt. Wildcat.
Above each fire-seared canyon, dark and steep,
On sun-soaked sand, on glare of shadeless slopes,
The silver seed sifts down where wind would heap
But snow of ash. . . . O, green and tendrilled hopes,
Uncoil your way through granite's hair-thin cleft,
Bind clay and sand, achieve a weather-hold
For small green plumes of summer, petal-drift
Of future springs . . . fawn beds on oak-leaf mold!
And, oh, come rain, soft rain, cool-fingered rain
To heal this scar of fire, wake grass again!

Maude Rubin

THE COMING OF SPRING

How do I know that spring is here?
Because the world is full of cheer.
The crocuses and daffodils
Peep out from all the window sills;

The grass is getting soft and green;
The garden makes a pretty scene—
Forsythia bushes all unfold
And show their blooms of fairy gold;

The tulips of my garden wall
Are getting beautiful and tall;
The birds are coming back to stay
And serenade us every day.

The world is full of joy and cheer!
That's how I know that spring is here!

Carmen Lagos Signes

SPRING

Skies are such a lovely blue;
    Grass is getting green;
Meadow is a cloth of gold,
    Waiting for the Queen.

Fields are bright with daffodils,
    Bluebirds on the wing;
Little brooklets run along,
    Keeping step with Spring.

Winifred C. Marshall

CHILD'S SONG IN SPRING

O Bluebird and Robin,
　　O Catbird and Wren,
I want you to rent
　　Our birdhouses again.

I'm lonely all winter
　　When you've gone away.
Your song is as welcome
　　As flowers in May.

S. Myrone McGinley

BIRD SONGS

Oh, there's music
　　In the forests
And there's music
　　In the glen
As the birds
　　Are warbling greetings
To the spring
　　That's come again.

All their piping
　　Is so merry
That the woodlands
　　Seem to ring
With the praises
　　Of the bird songs
For the coming
　　Of the spring.

Join the joyous
　　Woodland chorus
And raise high
　　Your voice in cheer—
Join the bird songs
　　In thanksgiving
For the springtime
　　Of the year.

Anonymous

86

FOR RENT

All winter the bird folk have lived in the South,
　　But now with spring sunshine and rain
They're looking for signposts that lead to the North,
　　And soon we shall see them again.

Some pleasant birdhouses I've put up for rent—
　　Bird tenants, I hope, come along,
For this is the sign I have put at each door:
　　These cottages rent for a song.

Leland B. Jacobs

THE BLUEBIRD

"Dear little blossoms down under the snow,
You must be weary of winter, I know;
Hark, while I sing you a message of cheer;
Summer is coming and springtime is here!

"Little white snowdrop! I pray you arise;
Bright yellow crocus! come, open your eyes;
Sweet little violets, hid from the cold,
Put on your mantles of purple and gold;
Daffodils! Daffodils! say, do you hear?
Summer is coming and springtime is here!"

Emily Huntington Miller

THE RETURN

A new note of joy from the orchard,
A glimpse of a vest reddish-brown
A little gray head cocked sideways—
Sir Robin has come back to town.

He seems to be glad that I notice,
As I watch for his lady's down,
And call out to others in gladness,
"Sir Robin has come back to town."

Though Winter is ruddy and jolly,
Miss Spring is the maid of renown—
And our hearts sing a glad song of welcome
When the Robins have come back to town.

M. Lucille Ford

SPRING'S HERALD

"I wonder," said the Crocus Bulb,
  "If it is time to grow;
It seems I've slept a long, long time
  Here in the ground below."

"I'm ready, too," said Daffodil,
  "To reach up toward the sun.
Come, let us go together—
  To go in two's is fun."

"You'd better wait and let me see,"
  The Pussy Willow said,
"If it is warm enough for you
  To venture on ahead.

"You're much too frail to take the risk,
  While I've a suit of fur;
If I should find that spring's returned
  I'll send you word to stir."

So Pussy climbed out on his branch,
  And then one bright spring day,
"Come up, the world's expecting you,"
  He telegraphed their way.

Mabel Niedermeyer

DISAPPOINTMENT

My father has a catalogue,
A jolly flower catalogue,
With what he says are pictures of all the latest flowers—
Of pansy kitten faces,
And posies edged with laces,
And bells to ring for four o'clock but not the other hours.

I've studied Father's catalogue,
This latest flower catalogue,
I must confess I don't believe it's right up to the minute,
For I've hunted hours and hours
To find my favorite flowers,
And there's not a purple thistle or a dandelion in it!

Leland B. Jacobs

SPRING COSTUME

Our wee apple tree
  Is the prettiest thing;
She dressed herself up
  In her nicest this spring.

She put on a gown
  Of shimmering green,
The laciest gown
  That I ever have seen.

And then in the night,
  With the greatest of care,
She put diamond dew
  On the flowers in her hair,

Those lovely pink blooms,
  With a perfume so sweet;
The rest of the orchard
  All knelt at her feet.

Marian Stearns Curry

SPRING GARDEN

The small brown bulbs I planted
  Beside our garden wall
Now bloom, like Cinderellas,
  All ready for the ball.

In silken gowns attired,
  As pretty as you please,
Coquettishy they curtsy
  To every princely breeze.

Leland B. Jacobs

WAKING UP

A little bean baby
Jumped out of bed,
With a white nightcap
Upon his wee head.

He yawned and stretched
In the warm, sunny air,
Till his cap tumbled off
His shiny green hair.

Irene M. Crofoot

JACK'S SECRETS

Jack-in-the-Pulpit, straight and slim,
Said not a word when I spoke to him.
With the peak of his funny hood pulled low,
He just pretended he did not know
That three new violets, white and sweet,
Hid in the moss at his very feet.
There was fringed polygala up the trail;
A bluebird sat on an old fence rail;
A flicker looked from a hole in a tree;
He had a secret no one could see.
But Jack-in-the-Pulpit knew quite well
Why Bellwort tilted her long white bell,
What the brook was saying with whispering sound,
What sunbeams wrote on the velvet ground.
Oh, that sly little chap in the funny hood
Knew all the secrets up in the wood,
Though he stood so mute and straight and slim,
And said not a word when I spoke to him!

Mabel S. Merrill

CROCUS CHILDREN

Just a little crocus
    Growing in the grass
Can announce the springtime
    To the folks that pass.

Just a little maiden,
    And a laddie wee,
Can spread joy and sunshine
    Where they chance to be.

Alice Crowell Hoffman

PUSSY WILLOWS

On slender willow branches,
    In little coats of gray,
You sway in springtime's breezes
    Like kittens at their play.

Where do you stay all winter?
    Your ways are very queer,
But when I see you, Pussy,
    I know that spring is here!

Mabel F. Hill

TULIPS

In the garden
    Tulips grow
Straight and golden
    In a row.
Each one holds its
    Empty cup
Drinking rain and
    Sunshine up.

V.W. Lachicotte

SPECIAL PRIVILEGE

My mother has a rosebush
Out by the garden gate.
Each day I count the buds on it—
Today I counted eight.
Tomorrow they'll be open,
All wide and sweet and pink;
And I may stand on tiptoe
And smell of them, I think.

Dorothy H. Gallagher

DANDELIONS

Last night a fairy strayed our way
    And played upon the lawn.
She danced and skipped from end to end—
    Then suddenly was gone.

What frightened her, I do not know,
    She dropped her purse and ran,
Leaving a wealth of golden coins
    To shine when day began!

Hazel Cederborg

GAY TULIPS

Red and yellow tulips
    Standing up so straight
Brighten up the pathway,
    Leading to the gate.
And when breezes kiss them,
    Gracefully they sway,
Happy in the sunshine,
    Welcoming the day.

Mollie B. Herman

OUR GARDEN'S
FLOWER PARADE

Our garden's been having a flower parade,
And, oh, what a splendid exhibit they made.

The bluebells kept ringing the place and the date,
The marigolds beamed at the garden gate,
While the hollyhocks marched in a column straight
  In a dazzling flower parade.

The garden parade was, indeed, a delight
With daisies pirouetting in yellow and white,
And acrobat roses that climbed out of sight
To the top of the trellis with no sign of fright.
  What a thrilling flower parade!

Though I missed the bands and the music they played,
I stood quite entranced at the flower parade.

The pansies and I didn't move from our place,
And I knew from expressions on each pansy face
That they all approved of the delicate grace
  Of our garden's flower parade.

Leland B. Jacobs

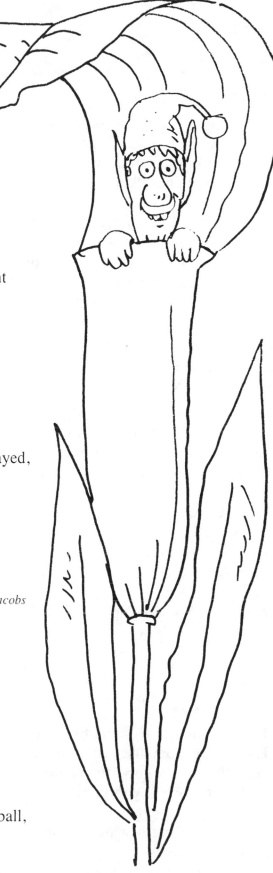

TULIPS

The tulips that bloom by the old garden wall
I play are fine ladies, all dressed for a ball.

Some wear fluffy ruffles of yellow or white,
While others wear crimson or orange so bright.

If they're caught in a shower on their way to the ball,
The rain does not hurt their silk dresses at all;

They're washed in dewdrops and dried in the sun;
To wear rainproof dresses, I think, must be fun.

Winifred C. Marshall

TOMMY

I put a seed into the ground
And said, "I'll watch it grow."
I watered it and cared for it
As well as I could know.

One day I walked in my back yard,
And oh, what did I see!
My seed had popped itself right out,
Without consulting me.

Gwendolyn Brooks

LITTLE SEEDS
WE SOW IN SPRING

Little seeds we sow in spring
growing while the robins sing,
give us carrots, peas and beans,
tomatoes, pumpkins, squash and greens.

And we pick them,
one and all,
through the summer,
through the fall.

Winter comes, then spring, and then
little seeds we sow again.

Else Holmelund Minarik

SEEDS

I planted shining seeds this spring—
   Just tiny seeds they seemed to be.
And yet I hoped so very much
   That they would change to flowers for me.

Today I saw a mist of green.
   It made me very happy, so
I said a little thank-you prayer
   To God, who made my flowers grow.

Winnifred J. Mott

THE SUN

The sun calls little seeds to come;
They wake from sleep and grow.
Sunlight is very good for them,
And good for us, you know!

It warms the Earth which circles it;
It gives the world its light.
When it rises, we have *day*.
And when it sets, there's *night*.

Mary Lou Healy

TINY SEEDS

Tiny seeds are everywhere
   Out of doors today.
Some have strong though airy wings
   To take them far away;
Some in cradles soft and brown,
From the trees to earth drop down,
Seeking for their winter's nap
   A soft, dark place to stay.

Vera L. Stafford

THE MINUET

Music-master Mozart wrote
Tiptoe tunes,
Elegant as flourishes
On polished silver spoons.
  With a bow low,
  Join hands,
  Step about and hold.
    Shoe buckle,
    Shirt ruffle,
    Brocade of gold,
      Flirting fans of sandalwood
      Whisper
      And unfold.

Music-master Mozart strummed
A rosewood harpsichord
While stiff on chairs of damask
Sat many a listening lord.
  With a ripple up,
  A trilling down,
  Ring chime ring,
    The harpsichord—a cage wherein
    A thousand linnets
    Sing. . . .

                    Claire Boiko

THE BRASS FAMILY

The mother is a round French horn
  With voice that's clear and sweet.
She very seldom solos,
  But two are quite a treat.

The father is a tuba tall.
  His music—puffs of sound.
In band or orchestra he's "tops,"
  His notes are full and round.

The daughter is a slide trombone
  With bell both loud and clear,
But she can wear a fitted mute
  For tones you scarcely hear.

The son is a bold bugle.
  He has a history
Of glorious martial music
  Which includes the reveille.

                    Mabel B. McGuire

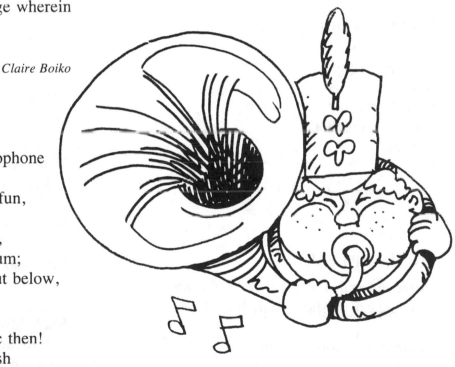

HOME-STYLE BAND

When Mother takes her saxophone
  And Father his guitar,
We children run to join the fun,
  No matter where we are.
Joanna plays a tuning chord,
  And Clifford beats his drum;
Then Father says, "Look out below,
  For here we come!"

You ought to hear the music then!
  You'd like to hear me dash
My cymbals on each other 'til
  They clash! clash! clash!
I never want to stop, you know,
  For, oh, it is so grand
To clash and clash the cymbals in
  Our home-style family band!

                    Marion Upington

91

MY MOTHER

I like the way
My mother talks.
I like the way
She laughs and sings.
And oh, I like the way
The way she walks,
As if her feet
Had kind of wings!

Barbara Young

MOTHER'S DAY

I'd like to buy Mother
Some perfume.
I'd like to buy Mother
A ring,
But I am too small
To have money,
And so I can't *BUY* her
A thing.

But Mother once told me
She's happy
Just seeing me laughing
And gay—
So I'll be especially merry
When Mother's Day
Comes,
In May.

Vivian G. Gouled

MEASURELESS

There are miles to measure countries,
  There are bushels, too, for wheat;

There are fathoms for the ocean,
  Degrees to measure heat.

There are years to measure ages,
  Light-years for stars above,

But no way has been discovered
  To measure mother love.

Alice Crowell Hoffman

MOTHERS ARE THE SAME EVERYWHERE!

"Eat your liverwort, my darling,
  And drink your milkweed up!"
Says Mama Elf to Baby Elf.
  "Here is your buttercup.
Stop blowing trumpet flowers, pet,
  Don't pull the cattails. No!
Just let the pussy willows be
  And let the dogwood go!
You'll never catch a dandelion
  Or tiger lily big,
If you eat only candytuft
  Just like a little pig!"
(I'm acting like a snapdragon?)
  "Now, where's my lady's-slipper?
I am not playing games, my child.
  You eat, you naughty nipper!"

Frances Gorman Risser

MY OWN MOTHER

She's always sewing buttons on,
  Or mending things I tear;
Whenever I come home from school
  I always find her there.

She's always doing little things
  That please me very much,
Like making cakes and planning trips
  To parks and zoos, and such.

She's always reading stories, too,
  Or teaching me a game;
And whether I've been good or bad,
  She loves me just the same.

Are you surprised that I find her
  Dearer than any other?
I'm sure by now you know her name.
  Of course—she is my mother!

Marian Kennedy

AN INFORMATION BUREAU

An information bureau right in our home you'll find.
Of course it is our mother, so loving and so kind.
For she's the one we go to; a question each one brings.
We're sure that she can tell us just where we left our things.
"Where is my hat?" That's Father; and Jack's mislaid a book.
"I've lost my specs," calls Grandma. "Please, will you give a look?"
"Where is my scarf?" asks Sister. "I left it in the hall."
And Dave comes in demanding, "Where's that new tennis ball?"
"Where are my gloves?" says Grandpa. "I need them right away."
"I've lost my notebook, Mother. I had it yesterday."
An information bureau, yes, really that is so;
We always go to Mother, and Mother seems to know.

Blanche Sprague

EXPLAINING IT TO DOLLY

I've tried my very best to be
    As good to you, dear dolly,

As Mother dear has been
    To Bud and me and Polly—

But if I have not measured up
    In one way or another,

You must remember it's quite hard
    To be as good as Mother.

Alice Crowell Hoffman

FLOWERS FOR MOTHER

I never have a special day
    To give flowers to my mother;
I give them to her every day
    To show how much I love her.

When I sweep the kitchen floor,
    Or care for baby brother,
Run on errands, or make the beds,
    I'm giving flowers to Mother.

It's lots of fun pretending
    And to hear my mother say,
"Thank you, dear, for all the flowers
    You've given me today."

Clara Rader

MOTHERS ARE FOR . . .

Mothers are for loving you
   If you're good or bad.
Mothers are for sharing
   Whatever makes you glad.

Mothers are for laughing
   At your favorite jokes.
Mothers are for helping you
   Get on with other folks.

Mothers are for telephones
   When they ring.
Mothers are for pushing
   When you're on a swing.

Mothers are for learning
   All the latest tunes.
Mothers are for sweeping
   All the dusty rooms.

Mothers are for feeding
   The cat when you forget.
Mothers are for scolding
   When your feet are wet.

Mothers are for baking
   Yummy birthday cakes.
Mothers are for nursing you
   When your tummy aches.

Mothers are for reading
   Stories old and new.
Mothers are for judging
   Between the false and true.

Mothers are for watching
   When you give a play.
Mothers are for clapping
   In a happy sort of way.

Mothers are for scrubbing
   And keeping all things neat.
Mothers are for cooking
   Delicious things to eat.

Mothers are for cuddling you
   When you have to weep.
Mothers are for covering you
   When you fall asleep.

Mothers are for teaching
   You to be polite.
Mothers are for hearing you
   Say your prayers at night.

Mothers are for washing
   Clothes in the machine.
Mothers are for ironing
   Them when they are clean.

Mothers are for loving
   When you snuggle up so tight.
Mothers are for kissing you
   A sweet and kind good night.

Dorothy Hewitt

MOTHERS

Mothers come in all sizes—from mini to maxi.
Some drive convertibles and others take a taxi.

Their hair comes in many different shades—especially reds—
On different—and even on the same—heads!

Complexions vary from palest vanilla to darkest chocolate.
There are old-fashioned mothers and ones who belong to the jet set.

Thousands of languages are spoken on this earth
And mothers speak all of them. (Sometimes for all they're worth!)

Some mothers have several academic degrees and others have never been to school.
Most mothers are tender and loving but some have been known to be cruel.

There are mothers who go out to work and ones who stay home all day,
But most mothers, most of the time, are "too busy to play."

No matter how different mothers are and always have been—
There's one thing they all have in common—and that's CHILDREN!

Ruth Birdsall

HIGH FLIGHT

Oh, I have slipped the surly bonds of earth,
And danced the skies on laughter-silvered wings;
Sunward I've climbed and joined the tumbling mirth
Of sun-split clouds—and done a hundred things
You have not dreamed of—wheeled and soared and swung
High in the sunlit silence. Hov'ring there,
I've chased the shouting wind along and flung
My eager craft through footless halls of air.
Up, up the long delirious, burning blue
I've topped the wind-swept heights with easy grace
Where never lark, or even eagle, flew;
And, while with silent, lifting mind I've trod
The high untrespassed sanctity of space,
Put out my hand and touched the face of God.

Pilot Officer John Gillespie Magee, Jr., R.C.A.F.

MEMORIAL DAY PARADE

The band is coming down the street.
The trumpets flash and shine.
The flag is waving out in front.
There are tingles up my spine.
Left. Right. Root-de-toot.
The bugles give the call.
Left. Right. Trum-de-dum.
The drummers march so tall.

The leader blows his whistle hard.
He gives his stick a spin.
Then every horn begins to play.
There are goose bumps on my skin.
Left. Right. Beep-de-beep.
The Navy's marching by.
Left. Right. Give a clap.
An airplane zooms the sky.

See the Gold Star Mothers.
They're riding on a float.
And now the soldiers come in view.
A lump is in my throat.
Left. Right. Hup-two-three.
A rhythm's in my feet.
Left. Right. There they go.
My heart just skipped a beat.

Blanche Boshinski

COURAGE OF LIFE

Without belittling the courage
    with which men have died,
We should not forget those acts of courage
    with which men . . . have lived.
The courage of life
    is often a less dramatic spectacle
    than the courage of a final moment;
but it is not less a magnificent mixture
    of triumph and tragedy.

John F. Kennedy

DAY OF MEMORIES

This is a day of memories
Of loyal hearts, and true,
    Of hearts that beat like ours today,
Of hearts that loved, of hearts that longed
    To live and sing, to work and play.

Now have come years of peace again,
Of lasting peace we pray.
    Still may we honor in our songs
That loyal band who for our land
    Died, hoping still to right its wrongs.

Emma W. Little

MEMORIAL DAY

It started right after the Civil War.
Our country was trying for wholeness once more.
Flowers were placed by an unmarked grave
To honor the fallen men, hardy and brave,
Whose lives had been given, our freedom to save.

Today, we will honor all brave men and true
Who fought to protect us—to guard me and you.
A freedom worth having, to keep it secure,
Takes a wide-awake heart and a hand that is sure
And a humble remembrance of what went before.

Mary Gray

MEMORIAL DAY

On Memorial Day
In peaceful May
We honor our soldiers—
The Blue and the Gray,
And other brave men
Who died for us
And kept our country
Victorious.

Ethel Jacobson

THE FIRST MEMORIAL DAY

May was green with grass and clover
and the tragic war was over.
Soldiers wearing blue and gray
had been buried where they lay.
But the states were torn apart.
What could heal the Union's heart?

In a dreamy Southern town
as the sun of May streamed down
women gathered flowers to strew
on the graves of Gray and Blue.
And the news spread far that day:
"Flowers for both the Blue and Gray."

More than words that rant and preach
flowers of springtime healed the breach.
For the men who fought and perished
fighting for the cause they cherished
were mourned alike—the Blue and Gray—
on that first Memorial Day.

Aileen Fisher

REMEMBERING DAY

All the soldiers marching along;
All the children singing a song;
All the flowers dewy and sweet;
All the flags hung out in the street;
Our hearts throb in a grateful way—
For this is our Remembering Day.

Mary Wright Saunders

MEMORIAL DAY

Memorial Day!
Exalted day!
Bringing memorial to all

Of gallant men,
True-hearted men,
Answering their country's call

With this quick cry:
"Here! Here am I,
Ready to stand or fall!"

In thought and deed,
Heroes indeed,
No fears their hearts appall;

And thus today,
Memorial Day,
Our heroes still enthrall!

Harriette W. Porter

Summer

End the school year on a high note with a poem to observe Flag Day, Father's Day, Independence Day. Then send off the class with thoughts of the circus, summer nights, the seashore, camping, swimming, hiking, and even summer bugs.

SUMMER'S INVITATION

Summer in a pleasant mood
At the school door smiling stood.
Smiling there she seemed to say,
"Come, it's time for rest and play;
Time for swimming and baseball;
Time to heed my cheery call
Off to hills and meadows free,
Off to woodland camp, or sea;
Time for hobbies specially planned
For vacation's wonderland;
Time for circus and parade;
Picnic time in park and glade."
In her pleasant restful way,
Summer beckons all today.

Leland B. Jacobs

SING A SONG OF SUMMER

When crickets sing
their evening song
and
fireflies turn
their lanterns on
and
spiders spin
at early dawn
and
weave their cobwebs
on my lawn—
    It's summer.

Kay Winters

JUNE FOURTEENTH

Can you tell why we celebrate
    This very special day,
And have you noticed waving flags
    All up and down the way?

The bands will play, the children march,
    And all the crowds will cheer.
It is the birthday of our flag,
    A day that we hold dear.

Winifred C. Marshall

RED, WHITE, AND BLUE

The red of the rose,
    The white of the snows,
The blue of the skies above,
    These colors three
    Are the ones we see
In the flag of the land that we love.

Ann McCune

A SONG FOR OUR FLAG

Sing for the flag,
Our country's flag!
We love its stripes and stars!
The stars of white on a field of blue,
The white and crimson bars.

Sing for the flag,
Our country's flag!
Emblem of liberty!
It floats above our beauteous land,
Protecting you and me.

Sing for the flag,
Our country's flag!
Oh, may it ever be
A brave and gallant symbol
Of truth and liberty!

Rachel M. Rolsheim

LUCKY STARS

I've often heard grown people say:
    "I thank my lucky stars!"
And wondered what they really meant,
    For Jupiter and Mars
Seemed much too far away, to me,
    For blessings to bestow.
But what they mean by "lucky stars"
    I think at last I know.

I see them shining every day—
    Morning, noon, and night.
Their whiteness gleams from out the blue,
    Brave champions of right,
They stand quite close in perfect rows,
    These fifty stars that shine.
They stand for union, purity,
    For courage, yours and mine.
For honesty and freedom
    Of speech and of the press,
For all the many principles
    Our nation's laws express.

So now I, too, can truly say:
    "I thank my lucky stars!"
And I will try to live my life
    So that it never mars
The qualities they stand for.
    The Banner of the Free
Shall always fly in freedom
    With lucky stars for me.

Carmen Lagos Signes

WHAT IS IT?

What blossoms like flowers
    in the middle of June?
What's inside at midnight
    and outside at noon?
What flutters in parades,
    marching to a tune?
It's a flag, flag, flag,
    on Flag Day in June.

Dorothy S. Anderson

98

OLD GLORY

The Star-Spangled Banner: Wherever it gleams,
At home or abroad, we behold, as it streams,
The symbol of liberty—message of hope
And freedom and light to the captives who grope
In the darkness, where tyranny reigns, iron-heeled,
And courage to those who would otherwise yield.
Our Star-Spangled Banner! To thee we'll be true,
Majestic Old Glory—the Red, White, and Blue.

In sacred emblazonry all may behold
Our liberty shining in every bright fold.
No fiery-eyed eagle or lion we see,
But only the beacon of loved liberty.
O'er Washington's army it blended its charms;
Before it Burgoyne once laid down his arms;
The flag floating o'er them, the patriots cheered;
The enemy shrank, for Old Glory they feared.

On the highlands at West Point its bright colors flew;
It floated o'er old Fort Montgomery, too.
When Arnold our fair country tried to betray,
Before it his treachery melted away.
Our army it cheered on its famous retreat;
To Valley Forge soldiers it brought courage sweet:
The Stars and the Stripes, as it floated on high,
Brought smiles to their lips and a tear to their eye.

At Trenton, the ice-rolling river it crossed;
At last over Yorktown in victory tossed.
Our immortal banner of red, white, and blue,
The blood of the brave was invested in you!
And we will defend you, come weal or come woe,
On land, on the sea, and wherever we go;
In health and prosperity, drought or in flood,
Because you were bought with the patriots' blood.

Ella Killam Bennett

OUR FLAG

I take great delight
In the glorious sight
  Of our flag.

I never grow tired
Of great songs inspired
  By our flag.

I feel my heart thrill
When the trumpets trill
  For our flag.

I salute the men
Whose allegiance has been
  To our flag.

I weep at the graveside
Of the soldier who died
  For our flag.

I think seriously
How I can worthy be
  Of our flag.

I see freedom anew
In the red, white, and blue
  Of our flag.

I pledge all my might
To keep the stars bright
  In our flag.

I pray God that He
Will in His majesty
  Bless our flag.

Betty Scott Baker

FATHER'S DAY

On Father's Day I try to see
How happy I can make Dad be;
I try to be just extra good;
And do each small thing as I should.

I'm extra helpful, thoughtful too,
And quick to see things I should do.
Then Dad grins, happy as can be
As he sits there and watches me.

So I think it would be fun
To make *each* day a happy one—
Have Father's Day not once a year,
But every day to hold it dear!

Grayce Krogh Boller

A TIE OF LOVE

I climbed on Daddy's knee and said,
"I know of something, brightest red,
With little spots of white and green,
And stripes of purple in between,
And if I could, that's what I'd buy
For Father's Day for you—a tie."

"A tie for me? Why, don't you know,"
My daddy answered, face aglow,
"I have one now that is just right—
A tie of love, that binds me tight;
But here's a gift I wouldn't miss."
And then he stooped and took a kiss.

Don Moon

DADDY'S STEPS

When Daddy walks along the street
And hurries home to me,
He takes the quickest, longest steps
That ever I did see.
But when I go to walk with him,
He acts quite diff'rently,
And takes the slowest, shortest ones
To keep in step with me.

Margaret Brown Elms

100

FATHER OF THE FUTURE

When Daddy was
A little boy
    He said he wished to be
The father of
A little boy—
    A little boy like me!

So, here I am!
And now I wish
    Someday when I grow tall
I, too, shall have
A little boy
    With whom I can play ball.

I'll take him to
The zoo, where I
    Shall buy him a balloon.
And when I am
A spaceman, we
    Shall both go to the moon!

Ilo Orleans

FISHING WITH DAD

Terry caught a bluegill,
Then Jerry caught one,
And I caught a bass.
But Daddy caught none!

Terry caught three more,
Jerry caught two,
And I caught the biggest one
Before we were through.

Oh, Daddy just rowed the boat,
And put on the bait,
And cast out our lines,
And got our tangles straight.

And he took off the fish.
(You never saw so many!)
And then he rowed us home.
And he never caught any!

Ethel Jacobson

SCHOOL

When school lets out in June, I feel
   As happy as can be.
I hop and skip and jump and run
   And shout and laugh with glee.
I'm sure that I will never want
   To go to school again,
But when September comes around,
   I always like to then.

Iva Riebel Judy

CLOSING DAY THOUGHT

I wonder if our schoolbooks are lonely all the day
While through the long vacations in cupboards put away?

I wonder if the blackboard seems rather out of place
Without a single piece of chalk to mark upon its face?

I wonder if the schoolroom is sometimes lonely, too,
While standing bare and empty without a thing to do?

But this we can assure them: When summer days all flee
We'll join them in September and keep them company.

Leland B. Jacobs

WHEN SCHOOL CLOSES

It's time to stand the books up
   In rows upon the shelves,
And pack the charts and posters
   In neat piles by themselves.

Collect the pens and pencils
   And put the ink away,
For schooltime now is over,
   And every day's for play.

Dorothy M. Baker

MY TEACHER, MY FRIEND

My teacher is a special friend.
She lifts a magic lantern high
And lights dark corners.
She holds the precious gift
Of knowledge in her hands,
And shares it with me.
She shows me the wonder of life,
The miracle of nature
And the mystery of science.
She opens a book,
And gives me the world.

Regina Sauro

CARRY ON

Our fathers braved the savage foe;
  they tamed the wilderness;
They starved and froze at Valley
Forge through months of storm and stress,
Their strength upheld by trust in
  Him, the God of righteousness.
    Their spirit still lives on.

They builded us a temple with foun-
  dations strong and sure;
They strove on many battlefields to
  keep our land secure;
They pledged their fortunes and their
  lives that freedom might endure,
    And we shall carry on.

Oh, help us face the perils and the
  darkness round about,
To guard against our enemies within
  and from without;
And banish from our hearts forever
  selfishness and doubt,
    That we may carry on.

We do not seek our lands or wealth
  or power to increase;
We only pray our country lead the
  way to trusting peace;
That strife and hate and tyranny
  throughout the world may cease.
    We vow to carry on.

Hold fast the precious heritage for
  which our fathers fought;
Defend the nation's strongholds
  which their sacrifice has bought;
Hand down the noble testament the
  patriots have wrought;
    And we shall carry on.

Mabel Lyon

I LOVE AMERICA

I love America:
  Her lakes and rolling seas,
Her wooded mountainsides,
  Her giant redwood trees!

I love America:
  Her fields of yellow grain,
Her villages and farms
  That stretch across the plains.

I love America:
  Her mountains bleak and grand,
Her highways smooth and wide
  That circle all the land.

I love America:
  She has so much to give—
Her churches, schools, and all
  Her homes where children live.

I love America:
  Her factories and planes,
Her rafts and boats and tugs,
  Her ships and streamlined trains.

I love America:
  From East to shining West,
For all she means to me;
  I love my country best!

Nona Keen Duffy

STRENGTH IN UNION

Many, many tiny threads,
  Each weak if used alone,
Woven tightly have become
  The finest banner known.
Many, many people, too,
  Of ev'ry walk and station,
Bound in love with purpose true,
  Make us a mighty nation.

Alice Crowell Hoffman

AMERICA

America, our Fatherland,
  We're loyal, brave, and true.
We love our country's valiant flag
  Of red and white and blue.

We love the freedom that we share
  From sea to shining sea.
We pledge our lives in full support
  Of our democracy.

Our continent is bountiful,
  With fruit and grain to spare;
Our land is blest with fertile soil
  And plenty everywhere.

We're all your loyal citizens,
  Our own dear Fatherland;
We love your verdant valleys fair,
  Your mountain peaks so grand.

We love our people and our land,
  Our homes and cities fair;
We love our own United States,
  In which we have a share.

Nona Keen Duffy

TO OUR COUNTRY

Our Country! As we look with pride
Upon this glorious land so wide,
  O may our every thought
Be to make you of greater worth,
An upright nation on the earth,
  Where justice true is wrought.

Our Country! As we watch each day
Thy banner in the breezes play,
  O may our every word
Be such as honest hearts would frame,
To bring honor to thy name,
  Where'er that name is heard.

Our Country! As we humbly share
In thy protection and thy care,
  O may our every deed
Be done to hold right standards high,
That freedom may not be a lie,
  But meet a people's need.

M. Lucille Ford

THERE'LL ALWAYS BE AMERICA

There'll always be America
  To stretch from sea to sea,
A land of liberty and love,
  A land so brave and free!

Let's help to build America,
  A land for future years,
A place where people may be safe,
  And free from grief and fears.

There'll always be America—
  Let's build her to endure,
Let's build for future citizens,
  And liberty ensure.

Let's help to build America,
  Let's serve her every cause,
Let's keep democracy alive,
  And help uphold her laws!

Nona Keen Duffy

103

FUN ON THE FOURTH OF JULY

Every year on the Fourth of July
We plan some fun, my sister and I;
Sometimes it's a picnic, sometimes a parade,
And Mom makes plenty of lemonade.

Year before last we had a parade
With floats the kids on our street had made.
We had a band with drums and things,
And colored balloons tied down with strings.

With flags that waved in the summer breeze,
We marched in step as nice as you please.
And folks on our street—young, old and bent—
Watched, as 'round and around the block we went.

The cross old man at the end of the street
Invited us in for a holiday treat;
And we were surprised, surprised as could be,
For he didn't like children, 'twas plain to see.

But when we were still, and maybe afraid
He said, "I had a boy once. He loved a parade.
I miss him most on the Fourth of July."
And we thought for sure he was going to cry.

And we like him now, for he isn't bad.
He is only lonesome, and old, and sad.
We ask him to fix our kites and toys.
He does it and calls us *his* girls and boys.

Anna K. Leonard

FOURTH OF JULY NIGHT

The fireworks are a lot of fun.
I watch each giant spark
As it goes streaking up the sky—
Then lights up all the dark
In a lovely splashing splatter
Of a thousand silver stars,
In a tumbling, rumbling clatter
That goes echoing off to Mars.

Eleanor Dennis

OUR AMERICA

This land of farms
With sowers, plowers,
Builders, dreamers—
This is ours.

This land of rivers
Fed by showers—
Hills and valleys—
This is ours.

This land of homes,
Gardens and flowers,
And happy children—
This is ours.

This land, where all
May share its powers
In peace and plenty—
This is ours.

This land of churches,
Pointing towers
Toward love and faith—
Thank God—is ours.

Elsie M. Fowler

THIS IS AMERICA

A land of mountains, lakes, and streams;
A land of prayers and hopes and dreams.
Mountains high, rivers wide,
Sunsets seen from the oceanside.
Busy cities, country towns;
Movie stars, and circus clowns.
A shady lane, a babbling brook,
A crowded street, a quiet nook.
Quarries, pastures, fertile land,
Forests green, and desert sand.
A clean wash on the line each Monday,
Public schools, and an ice-cream sundae.
  THIS IS AMERICA!
A land of mountains, lakes, and streams;
A land of prayers and hopes and dreams.

Hazel M. Thomson

LULLABY FOR SUMMER NIGHTS

Quietly hums
each breeze that passes
lullabies
in the trees and grasses
over and over
singing the words,
weaving a dream
for the tired birds,
hushing the nestlings
snuggled in trees,
and mice, and foxes,
and newborn bees,
and restless bugs
in hammocks of clover,
rocking, murmuring
over and over
lullabies in the treetops,
lullabies in the grasses!

Elsie S. Lindgren

SUMMER NIGHT

A summer evening's lovely
With its shadows blue and deep
And its busy crickets strumming
Drowsy songs to make us sleep.

With its flitting fireflies glowing,
With its stars so big and bright,
And its gentle breezes sighing
Little secrets through the night.

Jean Brabham McKinney

AFTER DARK

When darkness falls in summertime,
  The avenues of air
Are full of glowworm motor cops.
  They're zipping everywhere.

With flashlights snapping on and off,
  They signal: Left! or Right!
Directing Bugland traffic jams
  On highways of the night!

Frances Gorman Risser

AT EVENING

I like the little sleepy sounds
  You hear when day is done
When shadows gather here and there
  At setting of the sun.

A brook grows drowsy in the eve,
  As dusk comes still and slow;
You hear across the quiet night
  His murmur soft and low.

The wind no longer calls and shouts
  From high up in the trees;
He hums, instead, through evening hours
  His lulling melodies.

And little leaves that talk all day
  With wind and flitting birds
Speak now among the darkened boughs
  Their gentle whispering words.

So as the hours of sunset come
  And daytime noises cease,
The evening brings the weary world
  Its gifts of dreams and peace!

Arthur Wallace Peach

ROLLER SKATING

Roller skating
Is such fun;
I go almost faster
Than Bim can run.

He barks so close
I can't go straight;
I think he'd like
To roller skate.

Irene B. Crofoot

AWAY WE GO

Hippity-hop!
Skippity-skop!
We've hopped so long
Our feet won't stop.

We say hello
To those we meet
And hippity-hop
On down the street.

Eleanor Dennis

SHARING THE SWING

When I keep my swing all to myself
I can go as high as our pantry shelf.
When I share my swing with friend or brother,
And we take turns at pushing each other,
I go like the wind, away up high,
Till it seems as if I could touch the sky.

Alice Crowell Hoffman

MY AEROPLANE

My swing, my swing is an aeroplane.
  Up I go to see
The ground where bugs and creepers go,
Where grasses and the flowers grow.
  Alas, poor things, the ground's their chain.
  They cannot ride the aeroplane,
  The soaring, swinging aeroplane,
  Like me.

Unknown

JUMPING ROPE

See!
See!
See!
I'm jumping rope!
I'll jump
Fifty times
I hope!
I've jumped
Ten times.
I've jumped twenty.
I've jumped
Thirty times.
That's plenty!

Lee Blair

ROLLER SKATING

Swing, glide, sway and roll,
Watch for the cracks and jump the hole.
Over the walks, under the trees,
Skating along as fast as I please.

Clump, clump! over the grass,
Stepping aside for the ladies to pass.
Swing, glide, roll and sway,
Skating is fun on a sunny day.

Frances Arnold Greenwood

KICK A LITTLE STONE

Kick a little stone and it
Hops ahead of you—
The little stone is round and white
Its shadow round and blue—
Along the pavements, over the cracks,
The shadow bounces too:
A very friendly little sight
A cheerful thing to do.

Dorothy Aldis

ERRANDS

Roller skating, roller skating,
  On errands I can go
With a clatter, clatter, clatter,
  More often fast than slow.
Doing errands for the folks,
  While skating, makes it fun;
It's like playing while you work—
  A sort of two in one.

Iva Riebel Judy

107

A YEAR LATER

Last summer I couldn't swim at all;
I couldn't even float!
I had to use a rubber tube
Or hang on to a boat;
I had to sit on shore
While everybody swam.
But now it's this summer
And I can.

Mary Ann Hoberman

WHAT THEY ARE FOR

Curbstones are to balance on
Far from the ground.
Railings are to slide upon
And trees for running round.

Fences are for wriggling through,
Cracks and holes to hop,
And, though she does not like us to,
Puddles are to plop.

Dorothy Aldis

A HIKING CAUTION

Come let us hike, come let us roam,
But let's not leave our eyes at home.

All out-of-doors is overflowing
With things to see while we are going.

Gay birds on wing, and nests in trees;
Grasshoppers, too, and velvet bees.

Wild flowers fair and crawling creatures
That can indeed become our teachers.

Oh, let's be sure we're wide awake
The next time that a hike we take!

Alice Crowell Hoffman

GOING FISHING

I've got my fishing tackle
   And now that school is out,
I think I'll go a-fishing
   To catch a mess of trout.
I borrowed a big shovel
   From Jones's hired man.
I dug a lot of worms,
   And put them in this can.
See this great big fellow!
   Oh, boy, but he can squirm!
Any fish would bite, I guess,
   At such a juicy worm.
I found this good old pole,
   And then I bent this pin,
So now that I am ready
   I might as well begin.

Solveig Paulson Russell

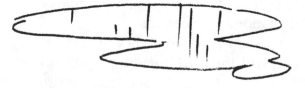

SATURDAY SECRET

Early in the morning,
way before eight,
I tiptoe out
and close the gate.

Only the birds
see me go
and they tell no one
that they know.

I climb high hills,
then roll right down.
I run through woods.
I walk near town.

I skip by streams.
I pat each tree.
I wave to deer
who wink at me.

I choose the flower
I like the most,
then hurry home
for jam and toast.

Everyone eats
and starts to talk.
Nobody guesses
my Saturday walk!

Mimi Brodsky

RACE

I'll race you
  to the corner.
I'll race you
  to the tree.
I'll race you
  to the driveway.
You
can't
beat
me!

B. J. Lee

ON A MOUNTAINTOP

You find wondrous things on a mountaintop.
You find trees and their cool spreading shade,
Birds, and the song which they sing all day long
And the nest-type homes that they've made.
And, if you will flush through the underbrush,
You may find a turtle who's sleeping
Or a wiggly worm or, of fiercer form,
A snake who is wriggling or creeping.
On the ground, there are prints—special-shaped dints—
Left by rabbit, by squirrel, or by quail—
Or perhaps by a bear. Better take care!
It's safer not to follow his trail.
There are rocks; there are stones
Of all sorts, shapes and sizes—
And hidden beneath them
All kinds of surprises—
The trail of the snail
Or the slimy old slug,
The ant who can't rest
Or the weird doodlebug.
There are all types of food (both bad and good)—
The mushroom, the toadstool—Beware!
Food that is found on the mountain's crown
Should always be checked with great care.
There's the scent of perfume from flowers which bloom
Deep-rooted in dark mountain loam.
There's the symphony of the fly and the bee
And the sound of the locust's dull drone.
There are breezes quite gentle and winds temperamental.
There is sunshine and sometimes some rain,
For what you find as you upward climb
You may never find ever again.
There are wondrous things on a mountaintop
Put there for me and for you.
But the most wonderful of all—watch out lest you fall!
Is a truly magnificent view.

Ann McCune

109

MY GARDEN

I'm planting a garden out of a book.
    It tells the most wonderful things:
How to spade up the ground and rake quite fine,
    How to straighten the rows with long strings,
How to fasten tomatoes up to a stake,
    How to shield tender plants from the sun,

How to put in beans with the "eye side" down—
    Oh, a garden will be such fun!
My book describes slugs and aphids and worms,
    It tells about purchasing seeds;
But one thing is lacking: the book does not say
    How to tell the plants from the weeds!

Laura Alice Boyd

OUR CIRCUS

Our circus is beginning now—
    That curly dog is Dick's;
The spotted pony is the one
    He rides for clever tricks.
The funny little polar bear
    Is really Baby Sue;
Though polar bears are timid,
    This one will wave at you.
The clown in suit of red and green
    Is quite well trained, you see—
Just watch him walk upon his hands;
    His name is Jimmy Lee.
The circus gave a big parade
    At one o'clock today.
Soon some ice cream we will buy
    With money that you pay!

Winifred C. Marshall

CIRCUS DAY IN OUR TOWN

At eight o'clock I went to see
The big top rising steadily.
The circus workmen, tanned and strong,
Made light their work with joke and song,
Till stood the tent, a splendid sight
Of poles and ropes and canvas white.

At ten o'clock the music played,
And down the street the long parade
Swung into view with blast and blare,
With elephant and dancing bear,
With clowns and all the circus joys
That thrill so many girls and boys.

At two o'clock in spirit gay
I saw the circus in full sway.
The lions roared, the ponies pranced,
The tightrope walkers turned and danced.
I clapped my hands and had to laugh
To see the clown and the giraffe.

Now when it's time to go to bed
The circus magic fills my head.
I still can hear the music played
And see the rings and the parade.
All night in dreams I hope I see
Each splendid circus memory.

Leland B. Jacobs

PLAYING CIRCUS

Old Shep made the dandiest camel
    (we tied a hump on his back),
While Patty and Mary rode horses
    (they pranced along down the track),
And the cat was a Bengal tiger!
    (We had to pretend he was wild,
For Mouser just wouldn't play circus.
    He went purring along, meek and mild.)

Johnny Blake and I were an elephant
    first; then he was a funny clown
And I was the circus man with a whip
    who keeps cracking it up and down.
When we marched around past the
    window and Mother saw our parade,
She came out with a platter of cookies
    and a pitcher of pink lemonade.

Inez George Gridley

LEMONADE IN THE SHADE

What is so nice, on a day in June,
As to stir up some ice with a long-handled spoon?
To sit in a sycamore's spreading shade—
With a glass of nice cool lemonade?
Oh, the hammock, we think, is lots of fun,
And the tree house suits most everyone—
But there must be ice and a long-handled spoon
To sip and stir, on a hot afternoon.
Now some prefer to race and run—
And wrestle and tease in the broiling sun—
Not me! There's nothing half so nice
As lemonade with lumps of ice—
To slowly stir, in the month of June,
Around in a glass, with a long-handled spoon.
Now Grandma likes her rocker and fan,
And Sister scoots for the ice-cream man—
But I only ask for a spot of shade,
And a tall, cool glass of lemonade
To sip and stir with a long-handled spoon
In the hot and heavenly month of June!

Jacqueline Rowland

ON SUMMER DAYS

On summer days I'd like to be
   A walrus in a frozen sea;
I think it would be very nice
   To play "I spy" through holes of ice.

Eddie W. Wilson

AT THE ZOO

Bobby went to the zoo one day,
   To see all the animals there.
He saw a giraffe and a kangaroo,
   A gorilla and polar bear.
But he stayed and he stayed at the monkeys' cage
   As though he would never be through.
   They gamboled and pattered
   They clambered and clattered—
   The funniest things at the zoo.

He saw a yak, with its silky hair,
   Zebras and leopards and deer;
An armadillo all covered with scales,
   Which he thought was very queer.
But oh, the monkeys! the gay little monkeys
   With their merry hullabaloo!
   That frolicked and tumbled,
   And chattered and mumbled—
   The liveliest things at the zoo!

He saw a hippopotamus fat,
   Elephants vast in size,
Chamois, hyenas, tigers, and apes,
   And camels with scornful eyes.
But Bobby's heart was with none of these!
   What thrilled him through and through
   Were the queer little monkeys,
   The *dear* little monkeys,
   The monkeys he saw at the zoo!

Lena B. Ellingwood

MAKE BELIEVE PARADE

After a circle
   We had made,
We marched around
   In a big parade.

With our make-believe
   Horns and drums in hand,
We all pretended
   To be a band.

And then we pretended
   A circus ring—
I was the lion!
   I was the King!

Leland B. Jacobs

THE CIRCUS PARADE

I like to hear the patter of the circus horses' feet,
As they come prancing gaily down the middle of the street.

I wish that I could dress in red and on a pony ride
With a plume upon my hat and bright buttons down my side.

I'd sit just like a queen and straight ahead I'd stare
At the pretty gilded cages of the tiger and the bear.

But every now and then I would bow my head, to greet
The great crowds of people that lined the busy street.

Rose Leary Love

SONG OF THE CALLIOPE

"Follow me! Follow me!"
   Sings the circus calliope.
"The circus is here. It's come to town
With its animals wild and its funny clown.
You'll hold your breath and you'll lose your hats
As you watch the tumblers and acrobats.
You'll be amazed at the jugglers' skill;
The high-wire artists will give you a thrill.
There's a flying trapeze and a Wild West Show!
Come on, everyone! Let's all go—
Let's go the circus. Follow me!"
   Sings the circus calliope.

Ann McCune

THE CIRCUS

Round and round the elephants plod,
The monkeys swing on a shining rod,
Bespangled ponies cavort and prance,
Roly-poly bears do a clumsy dance.
A peddler lifts up his voice to sell
Fresh roasted peanuts in the shell.
The acrobats whirl and loop the loop,
A dog jumps through a flaming hoop.
The circus is a sawdust flower
That blooms for an enchanting hour!

June Griffin Wrobleski

BUYING BALLOONS

Here comes the man
   Who sells balloons.
Some are as big
   And round as moons.
Red and yellow,
   And green and blue,
Purple, orange,
   And silver, too.
Get your money;
   We'll each buy one.
I'll take the red.
   Oh! it's such fun!
Blue and yellow
   And silver moons.
Here comes the man
   Who sells balloons.

Winifred C. Marshall

A LOST BALLOON

Tonight, if you notice
   A small, small moon,
I know it will be
   My silver balloon.

I bought one today
   At a circus stand,
And all of a sudden
   It slipped from my hand.

It will look lovely
   Tonight, but, oh!
If you know how to get it,
   Please let me know!

Elaine V. Emans

CIRCUS

The brass band blares,
The naphtha flares,
The sawdust smells,
Showmen ring bells,

And oh! right into the circus ring
Comes such a lovely, lovely thing,
A milk white pony with flying tress,
And a beautiful lady,
A beautiful lady,
A beautiful lady in a pink dress!
A red-and-white clown
For joy tumbles down,
Like a pink rose
Round she goes
On her tip-toes
With the pony under—
And then, oh, wonder!
The pony his milk-white tresses droops,
And the beautiful lady,
The beautiful lady,
Flies like a bird through the paper hoops!

Then he waggles his feet and stands on his head,
And the little boys on the twopenny seats
Scream with laughter and suck their sweets.

Eleanor Farjeon

THE CIRCUS

The circus came to our town!
   There was a grand parade!
I held on tight to Daddy's hand,
   I was *almost* afraid!

The lions looked like great big cats
   In their cage with golden bars;
A lady rode a barebacked horse,
   Her dress all bright with stars.

The elephants were very large—
   They nearly shook the ground!
And oh, the steam piano made
   A loud and merry sound!

Myrtle G. Burger

MY CHOICE

I like the blowing banners
   That tower toward the sky;
I like the prancing ponies
   With their heads held high.

I like the dancing elephants,
   And bears, both black and brown;
But best of all I think I like
   The jolly circus clown.

He walks, he rides, he slips, he slides,
   He tumbles on his nose,
And merry shouts of laughter rise
   No matter where he goes.

When Father says that I shall be
   A lawyer of renown,
I smile and say, "I'd rather be
   The jolly circus clown."

Leland B. Jacobs

THE CIRCUS

The circus is:
   big,
      bright,
         brilliant,
            breathtaking;
   beautiful,
      bobbing,
         bouncy,
            bustling;
   blue,
      bliss,
         beaming,
            booming;
   blooming,
      blazing,
         bubbly,
            buzzing,
               BURSTING!

Mary Anne Magnan

Merry-go-round

MERRY-GO-ROUND

The rollicking, frolicking merry-go-round
Goes around and around and around,
And the tinkly, twinkly music plays
With a gay and a silvery sound.
The ponies kick their frisky heels
At the tinkly, twinkly sound,
As the rollicking, frolicking merry-go-round
Goes around and around and around.

If I had my choice each summer day
Of the spot where I'd like to be,
The rollicking, frolicking merry-go-round
Would be the place for me.
And all of the time that the music played
With its tinkly, twinkly sound,
I'd go riding around and around,
On the rollicking, frolicking merry-go-round.

Marian Kennedy

WHEN THE MERRY-GO-ROUND IS STILL

The merry-go-round was silent.
It was still as it could be;
But the animals were whispering,
"Come play, come ride with me."
And so, I rode upon a horse,
The fastest horse in town.
I climbed upon a donkey
And went bouncing up and down.
I sat upon an elephant
And tightly held the reins.
I rode a zebra and a lion,
And stroked their silky manes.
I rode a camel and a goat;
I rode a cuddly bear.
And no one ever bothered me,
For no one else was there!
I never had such fun before.
I'll go again, I will,
And ride my animal friends once more
When the merry-go-round is still.

Anita E. Posey

A JOLLY RIDE

The merry-go-round has come to town;
    Let's go for a jolly ride.

Here is the little gilded coach;
    Baby Betty can sit inside.

Bobby can ride on a tall giraffe,
    And Ted on a tiger bold.

Martha and Sue like ponies best,
    With the bridles of red and gold.

Round and around and around we go,
    To the merry jingling tune.

Nothing is ever quite such fun,
    As a merry-go-round in June.

Winifred C. Marshall

MERRY-GO-ROUND

Of all the things at the carnival place
The one that we like the best
Is the merry-go-round where the horses race
Forever and ever at furious pace
Till the ticket man lets them rest.

Passing the crowds of people we fly
As long as the music plays.
Again and again their heads go by,
As we gallop and gallop with reins held high
In a kind of happy daze.

And the road we travel leads up and down
While we follow the horse ahead
Over the hills to a make-believe town.
Then suddenly all the machines run down
And we slip to the ground instead.

Margaret Hillert

MERRY-GO-ROUND

I climbed up on the merry-go-round,
And it went round and round.
I climbed up on a big brown horse
And it went up and down.
Around and round
And up and down,
Around and round
And up and down,
I sat high up
On a big brown horse
And rode around
On the merry-go-round
  And rode around
On the merry-go-round
I rode around
On the merry-go-round
  Around
    And round
      And
        Round.

Dorothy Baruch

THE MERRY-GO-ROUND

Oh, the merry-go-round, the merry-go-round;
Its horses never touch the ground!
The music starts and away we go;
Our hats and hair and dresses blow!
Faster and faster on we ride;
We wave to the folks who stand outside.
Then all at once the music is slow,
And off the horses we have to go!

Frances Arnold Greenwood

ON THE MERRY-GO-ROUND

On the merry-go-round
I go round and around
and around and around
and play I'm a needle
on a great big record
full of songs
that have no sound.

Bonnie Nims

THE FERRIS WHEEL

Here's a delight with which none can compare,
The sky-riding wheel you see at the fair!

Over the treetops it carries you high,
Higher and higher, up into the sky—
Then it comes down in the flash of an eye!

What a delight to turn round and around,
As high as the roof and then low as the ground.

Turning and turning it reaches the top;
Down, down again to the ground it will drop!
Oh, how I wish that it never would stop!

Josephine Van Dolzen Pease

THE LITTLE BROWN ROAD

The little brown road
    That goes running along
Seems to be humming
    A holiday song.

It sings of the brooklet
    Where speckled trout splash,
Of gay flowery meadows
    Where butterflies flash.

"Come race me," it teases,
    And darts up a hill;
I think I could catch it
    If it would stand still.

Donovan Marshall

MOOSE CROSSING

"Here's a moose crossing.
Let's stop here
And watch him cross over."

"It might take a year,"
Said the boy's doubting father,
Clutching the wheel.
"Let's finish our journey
Then eat a good meal."

"What's the sign for
If there ain't any moose?"

"The sign is for tourists,
You gullible goose!"

Just then a moose snorted
And crossed like a streak;
The boy's eyes exploded.
Poor dad could not speak!

Wilbert Snow

ROAD SONG

A winding road, a side road
    Beckons and nods to me
It may go to the mountain,
    It may go to the sea;
But I must heed a summons
    That cannot be denied.
I must know where the road goes
And what's on the other side.

Alice Crowell Hoffman

THE ROAD

When we go riding into town,
The road goes up and the road goes down;

Round a corner where a sign says *SLOW!*
Over a bridge with the water below.

I like to watch the trees and sky
And the houses and barns that we go by;

I like the horses and pigs and sheep
And the cows that all the farmers keep;

But best of all is to look behind
And watch the road unwind and unwind.

I always think and I always say,
"Where does the road run when it runs away?"

Reba Mahan Stevens

AMERICA IS ON THE MOVE

America is on the move.
It's vacation. Time for fun.
Wheels roll along the highways
From Maine to Oregon.

There are station wagons, trucks, and cars—
And campers, quite a few,
As families spend vacations
In search of something new.

They hike in Minnesota woods
And mountain-climb out west.
They camp in redwood forests,
Where camping's at its best.

They swim in motel swimming pools
And fish the streams for trout.
And when they're rolling home again,
The rest are rolling out.

So America is on the move.
Highways are filled with cars,
And wheels keep rolling night and day
Across this land of ours.

Jane W. Krows

CAMPING

Summertime has come again
   And camping days are here,
With fishing, swimming, boating, too—
   The best time of the year.

We climb the trees and go on hikes,
   And all grow strong and brown.
Our friends will hardly know us
   When we go back to town.

We do not miss the telephone,
   The movies, or the cars,
When we can fish and hike all day,
   And sleep beneath the stars.

Winifred C. Marshall

COOKOUT

From the shadows
Stab of laughter,
Hot dogs now
And stories after.
Blazing pine knots,
Charring logs,
Juice is oozing
From the dogs.
Smoke keeps busy
Closing eyes,
Sparks chase stars
In peeping skies.
Icy backs
And well-scorched fronts—
Time for songs
Or campfire stunts.

Don Marshall

A DEER SURPRISE

Up in Maine
On Mt. Katahdin,
We were camping by a stream.
Early, early,
On one morning,
When the world was still half dream,
A little deer came stepping, stepping,
Quietly from tree to tree,
Eyes a-question,
Nose a-quiver.
I looked at her, she looked at me.
When I reached
My hand to touch her
She was gone with a flash of white—
But we shared
A magic moment
Hushed between the dark and light.

Ruth McKee Gordon

117

SONG OF A SHELL

I held a sea shell to my ear,
  And listened to its tale
Of vessels bounding o'er the main
  And all the ships that sail.
It sang of brilliant water flowers—
  The bright anemones
That bloom beneath the ocean waves—
  Tossed in from seven seas.

Each time I harken to this song,
  I hear the breakers moan,
And fancy that a warning bell
  Rings from a lighthouse lone.
No longer need I wish to go
  Where foam-capped billows swell,
For I've an ocean of my own
  Within this pearly shell.

Violet L. Cuslidge

NEW HOME

Today, at the seashore, I built a house
  With a terrace and stables wide;
It had strong shell walls, chimneys square and tall,
  And I hollowed it out inside.

Tonight a mermaiden, little and shy,
  Will come from the green sea caves;
She will take my house and float it away
  To a city under the waves.

Her tiny sea horses will find a home
  In the stables I built so well,
While she will move into the pretty house,
  And, oh, but she'll love to tell

How she found this house on the beach one night,
  And that's how it happens that she
Has the only ranch-style home to be found
  In the city under the sea!

Frances Gorman Risser

A WAVE

I sat on the beach and a beautiful wave
  Came tumbling right up to me.
It threw some pink shells on the sand at my feet,
  Then hurried straight back out to sea.

It ran away swiftly and leaped up in foam;
  It bumped other waves in its glee.
I think it was hurrying to gather more shells,
  To bring as a present for me.

Gussie Osborne

A SAND WITCH FOR A SANDWICH

I walked the beach on a sunny day
And soon found a shell with which to play.
I made a castle, I made a moat,
I poured in water to sail my boat.

I made a farm and a racetrack, too,
And then a figure that sort of grew
Taller and taller as I piled more sand.
Then I shaped a face with one wet hand.

Oh, what a face—with an ugly beak
And a tall, tall hat that came to a peak!
I looked with pride at my ugly witch,
While all around I dug a ditch.

To keep her safe from the incoming tide,
I dug it deep on every side.
The waves rolled in and then slid back.
I waited for their wet attack.

One little wave crept up the beach,
But my sand witch it could not reach.
One, two, three waves filled the ditch.
Another wave took a nip at the witch.

A whitecap pushed with all his might
And ate that witch in one big bite!
I laughed as the water swished round my feet,
For *sandwiches* are made to eat!

Emily Sweeney

AT THE SEASIDE

When I was down beside the sea
A wooden spade they gave to me
  To dig the sandy shore.

My holes were empty like a cup
In every hole the sea came up,
  Till it could come no more.

Robert Louis Stevenson

SITTING IN THE SAND

Sitting in the sand and the sea comes up
So you put your hands together
And you use them like a cup
And you dip them in the water
With a scooping kind of motion
And before the sea goes out again
You have a sip of ocean.

Karla Kuskin

THE WAVES

The little waves ran up the sand,
  All rippling, bright and gay.
But they were little robbers,
  For they stole the sand away,
And when they'd tossed it all about,
  They piled it in the bay.

One day, there came a clever man;
  He walked along the shore,
And when he saw the crested waves
  Creep higher than before,
Said he, "I'll build a harbor wall,
  And you'll come here no more."

So then he started working;
  Stone after stone he brought.
The little waves beat at the wall;
  By day and night they fought,
Their white hair streaming in the wind,
  Their manner quite distraught.

But when the wall was finished,
  Like other of their ilk,
They tiptoed round the harbor
  As sleek and smooth as silk,
And purred around the fishing boats,
  Like kittens lapping milk.

Gertrude M. Jones

Down in the meadow

MEADOW SURPRISES

Meadows have surprises,
You can find them if you look;
Walk softly through the velvet grass,
And listen by the brook.

You may see a butterfly
Rest upon a buttercup
And unfold its drinking straws
To sip the nectar up.

You may scare a rabbit
Who is sitting very still;
Though at first you may not see him,
When he hops you will.

A dandelion whose fuzzy head
Was golden days ago
Has turned to airy parachutes
That flutter when you blow.

Explore the meadow houses,
The burrows in the ground,
A nest beneath tall grasses,
The ant's amazing mound.

Oh! Meadows have surprises
And many things to tell;
You may discover these yourself,
If you look and listen well.

Lois Brandt Phillips

VACATION

Vacation's full of jolly things
Like butterflies with yellow wings
And flowers that nod with every breeze,
While squirrels bark from tall oak trees;

But I am sure you cannot guess
What gives me greatest happiness.
It's this: I like the grass so sweet
That cools and tickles my bare feet.

Eddie W. Wilson

SOUTH WIND

The days grow long, the mountains
Beautiful. The south wind blows
Over blossoming meadows.
Newly arrived swallows dart
Over the streaming marshes.
Ducks in pairs drowse on the warm sand

China, eighth century
Translated by Kenneth Rexroth

BUSY WORLD

Bees are buzzing, frogs are hopping,
   Moles are digging. There's no stopping
Vines from climbing, grass from growing,
   Birds from singing, winds from blowing,
Buds from blooming. Bees are humming,
   Sunbeams dancing, raindrops drumming.
All the world is whirling, dizzy—
   Summertime is very busy!

Frances Gorman Risser

SMELLS OF SUMMER

There are certain things in summer
That smell real nice to me.
The moss and ferns and woodsy things
I like especially.

The grassy lawn just freshly cut,
The fragrant stacks of hay,
The clean outdoors when it has rained,
The salty ocean spray—

Pine needles warming in the sun,
Fresh corn, and berries, too,
Bright flowers in a big bouquet—
I like these smells, don't you?

Vivian Gouled

120

TREE SHADOWS

I did not know how rare a sight
  A tree could be,
Until I spent a summer month
  Down by the sea.
On either side the sandy dunes
  The waves ran free,
And islands with white lighthouses
  Adorned the sea.
But when the sun's glare tired my eyes,
  I could not flee:
There were no grateful shadows made
  By leafy tree.
So now I dread to break a branch
  Grown by a tree,
Because I know how rare a sight
  Green shade may be.

Lucy M. Church

THE TREES' PLEAS

Man, watch match!
Bright sparks blow;
Twigs reach out;
Tree tips glow.

Man, stamp flame!
Wildflowers urge;
Save our stems,
Stem the surge.

Man, spare trees!
Won't you learn
Woods are lost
When we burn?

Kay Cammer

THE OAK

The oak stands straight
  and tall,
but not in boots,
nor any shoes at all:
just in roots.

Norma Farber

THE LADIES

In their gowns of silver,
  With parasols of green,

The ladies have gone walking
  In a pleasant scene.

Graceful is their bearing
  And gracefully they go,

With low-toned chat and comment,
  In a friendly row.

Sunbeams, golden-tinted,
  Before them touch the ground;

Their silken gowns in rustling
  Make a whispering sound.

I can see them strolling
  As from the road I look—

Six ladies who are really
  White birches by a brook!

Arthur Wallace Peach

TREES

Trees are for birds.
Trees are for children.
Trees are to make tree houses in.
Trees are to swing swings on.
Trees are for the wind to blow through.
Trees are to hide behind in ''Hide and Seek.''
Trees are to have tea parties under.
Trees are for kites to get caught in.
Trees are to make cool shade in summer.
Trees are to make no shade in winter.
Trees are for apples to grow on, and pears;
Trees are to chop down and call, ''TIMBER-R-R!''
Trees make mothers say,
''What a lovely picture to paint!''
Trees make fathers say,
''What a lot of leaves to rake this fall!''

Shirley Bauer

A TREE IS BEAUTIFUL TO SEE

A tree is graceful, straight, and tall,
Outlined against the sunset sky,
Its leafy branches lifted high—
A tree is graceful, straight, and tall!

A tree is beautiful to see,
When drenched with rain, its limbs droop low,
Or when they're heaped with falling snow
A tree is beautiful to see!

A tree is such a lovely sight,
When dressed in autumn red and gold
Or when its first buds unfold—
A tree is such a lovely sight!

Edna Jeanne Graham

MY TREE

O Tree, so big and stout and strong,
You've lived so very, very long;
A hundred years or more, I'm told,
And yet you're not so very old.

A hundred secrets you could tell
Of children whom you love so well,
Who came and sat beneath your shade
Or underneath your branches played.

A hundred birds have built their nests;
Your leaves have softly kissed their breasts;
Your branches seem to touch the sky,
Yet you were once as small as I.

Some day when I have grown up, too,
I'm coming back to visit you;
And changed though other things will be,
I'll find the same dear friendly tree.

Garnet Engle

FOREST FIRES

Someone dropped a burning match
Unheeded by the way;
It caught on fire some underbrush;
Its user did not stay.
From grass to brush, from brush to tree,
So stealthily it ran,
That no one ever guessed or knew
Just where that fire began.

Someone built a campfire
And failed to put it out.
A breeze came up and quickened;
The embers spread about;
And soon the woods were blazing.
The fire spread and spread;
The trees that took long years to grow
Stand blackened now and dead.

Someone saw a little fire
As he was passing by.
He did not stop to put it out;
He did not even try.
He had not started it, of course;
He had no time to spare;
That it might start a forest fire
He did not even care.

Myrtle Barber Carpenter

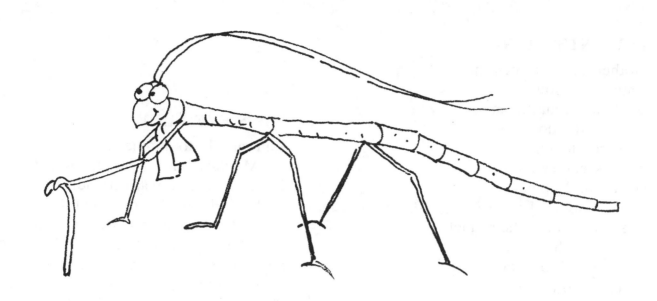

BEETLES IN THE GARDEN

Beetles
may be
large or small,
shaped from
flat to
humpy tall,
iridescent,
red or
yellow—
every one
is a hungry fellow.

Elsie S. Lindgren

THE INSECTS' WORLD

Insects are creatures with three pairs of legs.
Some swim, some fly; they lay millions of eggs.
They don't wear their skeletons in, but out.
Their blood just goes sloshing loosely about.
They come in three parts. Some are bare; some have hair.
Their hearts are in back; they circulate air.
They smell with their feelers and taste with their feet,
And there's scarcely a thing that some insect won't eat:
Flowers and woodwork and books and rugs,
Overcoats, people, and other bugs.
When five billion trillion keep munching each day,
It's a wonder the world isn't nibbled away!

Ethel Jacobson

BEETLES

Emerald, ruby, turquoise blue,
Beetles come in every hue:
Beetles that pinch or sting or bite,
Tiger beetles that claw and fight,
Beetles whose burnished armor gleams,
Whirligig beetles that dance on streams,
Antlered beetles in staglike poses,
Beetles that smell—and not like roses,
Others that click like castanets,
That dig or swim or zoom like jets,
Hard as coffee beans, brown as leather,
Or shimmering bright as a peacock feather!

Ethel Jacobson

A QUEER TWIG

Out in the woods I found today
    A queer thing, without doubt—
A wee twig that did not stay still,
    But tried to walk about.

I thought this tiny twig had planned
    To play a funny trick,
Until I learned it was a bug
    Known as the "walking stick."

Alice Crowell Hoffman

THE ANTS' PICNIC

Mother ants, brother ants,
Sisters and cousins,
Uncle ants, auntie ants,
Ants by the dozens,
Gathered together
In Larkfeather Lane
For a family picnic.
(Does it look like rain?)
They spread out their lunch
On a nice shady site
And all had just started
To take the first bite
When along came some people
Who plopped in a bunch
On top of the ant clan
And their picnic lunch.
The ants heard it thunder,
Then Grandfather Pete
Said, "Raindrops and people
Make picnics complete!"

Carol Quinn

FLY'S-EYE VIEW

Said one fly to another fly:
  "My dear, aren't people awful?
Their attitudes toward friendly flies
  Should be declared unlawful.
Why, if we compliment their food
  By tasting a small ration,
Some uncouth person's sure to go
  Into a senseless passion.
They walk about on grubby floors,
  Though they have lovely ceilings,
Which proves that human beings lack
  Our more artistic feelings!"

Frances Gorman Risser

FLIES

Flies
Have jeweled eyes,
Wings of gauze,
And tiny claws
That let them clamber,
Without reeling,
Upside down
On the ceiling!

Ethel Jacobson

A CENTIPEDE

A centipede was happy quite,
  Until a frog in fun
Said, "Pray, which leg comes after which?"
This raised her mind to such a pitch,
She lay distracted in a ditch,
  Considering how to run.

Author unknown

THE SPIDER

The spider loves to entertain
Her neighbors and relations,
But woe to any bugs or flies
Who accept her invitations!
So have a care, be wary of
This most accomplished spinner,
When she murmurs, "Be my guest!"
What she means is, "Be my dinner!"

Ethel Jacobson

SPIDER WEBS

The spiders were busy last night;
From every fence and tree
They hung their lacy webs
For all the world to see.

The mist was busy too;
In the stillness of the night
It strung the spider webs with pearls
To catch the morning light.

One spider wove a web
Like frost on a windowpane;
Another one spun a single thread
That looks like a jeweled chain.

Motionless hang the webs,
By the quiet sunbeams kissed;
A fairy world was made last night
By the spiders and the mist.

James S. Tippett

AN EXPLANATION OF
THE GRASSHOPPER

The Grasshopper, the Grasshopper,
I will explain to you:
He is the Brownies' racehorse,
The Fairies' Kangaroo.

Vachel Lindsay

THE SPIDER WEB

The spider spun a silver web
    Above the gate last night.
It was round with little spokes
    And such a pretty sight.

This morning there were drops of dew
    Hung on it, one by one;
They changed to diamonds, rubies red,
    When they were lit with sun.

A spider's nice to have around
    To weave a web so fine.
On which to string the drops of dew
    That catch the bright sunshine.

Truda McCoy

CRICKET SONG

The cricket sings
When shadows creep.
His evening song
Says, "Sleep . . . sleep."

I heard this song
From my warm bed.
"Sleep . . . sleep"
Is what he said.

Then very soon
I could not keep
My eyes awake,
So went to sleep.

When morning came
And skies were bright
The cricket's song
Was locked up tight.

But this I know:
When shadows creep,
He'll sing again,
"Sleep . . . sleep."

Elsie M. Strachan

TRUSTING BUTTERFLY

Hold your breath—
Don't come too near!
She's just about to land
   Ah!
A butterfly has honored me
By resting on my hand.

Birds fly from us great humans.
And beetles scuttle past,
Antennas quivering just as if
Each moment were their last.

How wise, how kind, she makes me feel!
For, pausing on her jaunt
From flower to tree,
She's choosing me
To be her confidant!

Claire Boiko

THE COCOON

I found a cocoon
That a caterpillar made,
Fastened to a leaf
Hanging in the shade.
He barely had room
To wiggle or wag,
Like me zipped up
In my sleeping bag.

I looked each time
That I passed his way
But he never budged—
Until just today
Something happened!
He wagged and wiggled
And then climbed out
And carefully jiggled
Small wet wings
That grew as they dried.
He'd turned to a butterfly
Inside!

Ethel Jacobson

AN EXPLANATION

I often think a butterfly
   With golden, shining wings
Most beautiful of all the earth's
   Wee flying things.

Sometimes I fancy that he is
   A sunbeam sailing 'round,
Flitting here and there so still
   He makes no sound.

And once I guessed how he is made:
   Upon his wings I saw
A diagram in black such as
   Someone might draw.

It looked as if whoever drew
   The lines had been in doubt,
And then was pleased, and so forgot
   To rub them out!

Arthur Wallace Peach

IF YOU WILL ONLY WAIT

The caterpillar said with a sigh,
to the bumblebee as it was flying by,
"If only I had wings as pretty as you,
I'd be very happy. Please tell me what to do!"

The bumblebee responded with a smile,
"If you will only wait a little while,
you'll be the happiest one in the sky,
because you'll be a pretty butterfly."

Carlotta Fuerstenberg

THE SWARM OF BEES

One little honeybee by my window flew;
Soon came another—then there were two.
Two happy honeybees in the apple tree;
One more bee came buzzing up—then there were three.
Three busy honeybees starting to explore
Another bee came to help—then there were four.
Four laden honeybees flying to the hive;
They were joined by one more bee—then there were five.
Five tired honeybees with the others mix;
Now there's a swarm of them—a hundred times six.

Elsa Gorham Baker

FIREFLIES

In the soft dark night
when the wind is still
and bullfrogs croak
at the bottom of the hill,
the fireflies reach
inside their coat pockets
and screw little light-bulbs
into their sockets
so they can fly
through the night and play
without bumping their heads
or losing their way.

Aileen Fisher

BEES IN THE TREES

I wonder if the bumble bees
    That buzz around our pepper trees
        Ever sneeze?

Hildred Bach

THE FIREFLY LIGHTS HIS LAMP

    Although the night is damp,
The little firefly ventures out,
    And slowly lights his lamp.

Unknown (Japanese)

ADVENTURE

One night a little firefly
    Was looking at a star,
And said—but no one heard him—
    "I wonder what you are."
Then, eager for adventure,
    And brave as he could be,
He trimmed his little lantern
    And flew away to see!

May Justus

RAIN ON THE WINDOW

WATCH!
 One drop
   starts
    slowly
     down—

then with a rush
joins a second,
picks up a third!

Now
 the big
  three-drop
   races
    to the
     bottom
      PLOP!

Elizabeth Searle Lamb

START OF A STORM

The trees
go wild,
yellow stabs
the sky,
awnings leap,
papers fly—
and suddenly,
with a rattling cry
against the pane,
roars
the rain!

Lou Ann Welte

GREAT LAKES STORM

How wild the lake!
How wild and gray!
The whitecaps leap
In spume and spray.
Unharnessed winds
Make billows roar.
They rush and break,
The skies grow black,
Sharp lightning strikes,
Loud thunders crack—
Now guard the dikes!
Down seeps the rain,
A blinding sheet!
High combers dash—
Sky, water meet.
The storm is spent—
Forth peeps the sun.
White-crested waves
Rush, break, and run.
Though skies may clear,
Swells roll all day.
Seagulls appear,
Sun gilds the bay.

Louise M. Diehl

SUMMER RAIN

What could be lovelier than to hear
   the summer rain
   cutting across the heat, as scythes
   cut across grain?
   Falling upon the steaming roof
   with sweet uproar,
   tapping and rapping wildly
   at the door?

No, do not lift the latch,
   but through the pane
   we'll stand and watch the circus pageant
   of the rain,
   and see the lightning, like a tiger,
   striped and dread,
   and hear the thunder cross the shaken sky
   with elephant tread.

Elizabeth Coatsworth

HEAVENLY SWEEPERS

After the rain,
The sky has a hosed-down look,
As though some heavenly santitation crew
Had rolled along,
Scrubbing the airy street
With generous streams of iridescent dew;
But leaving behind
Some careless clouds which flutter
Like crumpled paper
In the empyrean gutter.

Alice Briley

Anytime

Here are poems to help resolve self-image problems and motivate discussions of family and friends. Other poems can introduce a unit on pets, the history of travel, a project on city life, a look into the past, a study of words, more.

THE BIG LAUGH

I laugh,
You laugh,
We all laugh together;
Spring laugh,
Fall laugh,
A laugh for wintry weather;
Light laugh,
Dark laugh,
Night and morning laughter;
But it takes
The BIG laugh
To shake the roof and rafter.

Lee Blair

THE SMILE

A scowl and a smile
    Met each other one day;
But somehow the scowl
    Was not able to stay.
Facing the smile,
    It just melted away.

Winifred J. Mott

129

LOOK AT ME

Look at me!
It isn't showing.
You can't see it,
But I'm growing!

Ida M. Pardue

FRECKLES

Freckles are speckles,
Quite plain to see
On Ladybug,
Tiger Lily,
Butterfly—
And ME.

Mabel Watts

INSTANT EVERYTHING

Instant coffee, instant tea
That's the way it seems to be.

Rush to catch the bus for school.
Rush to give my Dad a tool.
Rush to get my lesson done.
Rush to go outside and run.

Gulp my meal so I can see
The early movie on TV.

Why are we in such a flurry?
Everybody's in a hurry.

I'd like to turn the world around
Reduce its speed and slow it down.

Like to sit awhile and think
Like to slowly sip a drink.

I couldn't do it if I try
The rushing world would pass me by.

Instant cocoa, instant tea
But there'll never be an "instant" me.

Jane W. Krows

FUTURE PLANS

My brothers and their playmates all
  Keep planning what they'll do
When they are very big and strong
  And educated, too.

John plans to be an engineer,
  And Carl a pastry cook.
And George will go to practice law,
  And Ben will write a book.

Tom says he'll be a carpenter.
  Don wants to be a cop.
And Bob will keep a grocery store
  Or else a candy shop.

They're all so full of business plans
  They won't have time to be
The president in Washington—
  Which leaves that job for me!

Harriette Wilburr Porter

QUIET

I can be as quiet as a spider or an ant,
Quiet as a butterfly;
  don't tell me that I can't.

I can be as quiet as a little fleecy cloud,
Quiet as a snowflake;
  now that isn't very loud.

I can be as quiet as a baby chick asleep,
Quieter than that!
  How quiet can you keep?

Walter L. Mauchan

EVERYBODY SAYS

Everybody says
I look just like my mother.
Everybody says
I'm the image of Aunt Bee.
Everybody says
My nose is like my father's
But *I* want to look like ME!

Dorothy Aldis

TWINS

I think it would be
Lots of fun,
If I were two
Instead of one.

I'd never be lonely
Outdoors or in,
For wherever I'd go
Would go my twin.

On birthdays Mother
Would always bake
Two—not one
Big birthday cake.

At night there'd be
Two soft little beds,
And two soft pillows
For two sleepyheads.

Oh, everything would be
Doubly nice,
If I could only
Be me twice!

Jean Brabham McKinney

GIANT

One foot in the river,
    One foot in the lake—
What wonderful strides
    A giant can take!

The water goes ''squish''
    When he wiggles his toes.
Oh, giants have fun,
    As anyone knows.

His red rubber boots
    Reach up to his knee.
Why, puddles are nothing
    To giants like me!

Elizabeth Sawyer

I TALK

Kittens mew,
Doves coo.

Birds cheep,
Chicks peep.

Lions growl,
Dogs howl.

Monkeys chatter,
Starlings clatter.

Ducks quack,
Hens clack.

Parakeets squawk,
But *I talk*.

Magdalen Eichert

JUMP OR JIGGLE

Frogs jump
Caterpillars hump

Worms wiggle
Bugs jiggle

Rabbits hop
Horses clop

Snakes slide
Seagulls glide

Mice creep
Deer leap

Puppies bounce
Kittens pounce

Lions stalk—
But—
I walk!

Evelyn Beyer

MY LOOSE TOOTH

I had a loose tooth, a wiggly, jiggly loose tooth.
I had a loose tooth, hanging by a thread.

So I pulled my loose tooth, this wiggly, jiggly loose tooth.
And put it 'neath the pillow when I went up to bed.

The fairies took my loose tooth, my wiggly, jiggly loose tooth.
So now I have a nickel and a hole in my head.

Ruth Kanarek

IN BETWEEN

I'm not the oldest.
I'm not the youngest.
It's no riddle.
I'm in the middle.
I'm not the tallest.
I'm not the shortest.
I can be seen,
Just in between.
I'm not the darkest.
I'm not the lightest.
My face and hair
Are just there.
I'm not the thinnest.
I'm not the fattest.
I'm just right
For my height.
I'm not the biggest.
I'm not the baby.
It is cozy to be
In the center of three.

This is not the end—
My very best friend
  is not the oldest
  or the youngest,
  the tallest
  or the shortest,
  the darkest
  or the lightest,
  the thinnest
  or the fattest,
  the biggest
  or the baby.
It's plain to see
She's sandwiched in between
Just like me.

Rose Cheroff

EXACTLY RIGHT

They say that I'm too young
To cross the street to play,
That I'm too old to cry
When I don't get my way,
That I am much too big
To swing on the garden gate,

But very much too small
To stay up after eight.
I'm young, I'm old, I'm big, I'm small—
Do you think, in age and height,
I will ever grow to be
Just exactly right?

Laura Arlon

WIGGLY TOOTH

Once I had a little tooth
That wobbled every day;
When I ate and when I talked,
It wiggled every way.

Then I had some candy—
A sticky taffy roll;
Now where my wiggly tooth was—
Is nothing but a hole!

Lillie D. Chaffin

THE BUTTON BOX

My grandmother's button box
Is a delight to see;
There are all sorts of buttons,
Each with a history.

There are the tiny buttons
That held Dad's clothes in place
When he was a little tad
Who liked to romp and race.

And then there are the buttons
Granddaddy wore on gray,
When he stood by Grandmother
Upon their wedding day.

There are dainty pearl buttons
That Mother used to wear,
When she was seventeen,
So pretty, young, and fair.

There are big wooden buttons
From Great-Grandfather's suit
And fancy brass ones he wore,
When he played the flute.

I love that old button box
When Grandmother sits with me,
And picks out all the buttons
With a family history!

Helen Kitchell Evans

I WOULDN'T MISS IT

I'm always in the kitchen
When Mother's there to bake,
Because I like to watch her
Spread frosting on a cake.

She does it very quickly—
It hardly takes a minute—
And then she lets me lick the bowl
That had the frosting in it!

Lucretia Penny

SISTERS

My sisters scold me every day
About my hair,
About my fingernails and shoes,

And they declare
That they would rather not be seen
Around with me.
I ask you, now: Is that the way
They ought to be?

But when I fell and hurt my knee
You'd be amazed
How jolly good they were to me.
They even praised
The way I didn't cry 'n' stuff—
Or bother Dad.
So, all in all, I guess that sisters
Aren't so bad!

Muriel Lumsden Sonne

BROTHERS

My brothers almost every day
    Would make me mad;
At last they all went off to camp—
    And I was glad!

I played around the house and helped
    My mom to bake;
And no one teased—or took the biggest
    Piece of cake.

And no one lashed my dollies to
    The lilac tree,
Or grabbed my things and hid them where
    I couldn't see.

But soon I missed their corny jokes
    And jolly noise—
Now I can hardly wait today
    To see the boys!

Muriel Lumsden Sonne

OUR GRANDMOTHER

Our Grandmother
Bakes homemade bread,
And is very handy
With needle and thread.

She lets out hems,
And darns and patches;
Sets the pills up high,
And hides the matches;

Corrects our grammar,
Calls good manners *art;*
Tells Bible stories
She knows by heart;

Grows African violets
In a dozen pots;
Baby-sits us
And likes us lots!

Mildred D. Shacklett

A HOUSE, A HOME

What is a house?
  It's brick and stone
  and wood that's hard.
  Some window glass
  and perhaps a yard.
  It's eaves and chimneys
  and tile floors
  and stucco and roof
  and lots of doors.

What is a home?
  It's loving and family
  and doing for others.
  It's brothers and sisters
  and fathers and mothers.
  It's unselfish acts
  and kindly sharing
  and showing your loved ones
  you're always caring.

Lorraine M. Halli

UNCLE FRANK

It's queer about my Uncle Frank,
He sits and figures in a bank,
When he might keep a candy store—
A shining sign above the door.
Or he might keep a big toy shop
With things that fly and skip and
hop—
With trailer trucks and things that
crank,
Instead of working in a bank.

Monica Shannon

GRANDPA'S GARDEN

My grandpa has a garden
  That never wilts or fades,
Although he never plows it up,
  Or waters it, or spades.

He never worries if it storms,
  Or fears the hottest sun;
And yet his garden's filled with plants,
  And he just loves each one!

He'll say to me, "Come, take a look.
  Now aren't those pansies sweet!
Oh, see this lovely hyacinth—
  And here's a marguerite!"

My grandpa's very feeble,
  For he's past eighty-nine
And yet his lovely garden
  Is always in its prime.

Yes, Grandpa has a garden
  Without scarecrow, fence, or dog;
And, all in lovely colors,
  Keeps it in his catalogue!

Sarah Grames Clark

FRIENDS

Tall friends, short friends,
Skinny and wide;
Red haired, black haired,
Side by side.

Old friends, young friends,
And in-betweens;
Moms and Grandpas,
Tots and teens.

From Washington
To Delaware,
Friends are found
Most anywhere.

It may seem odd
To think and yet;
Friends are strangers
You've never met!

Janet C. Miller

FRECKLES

Jerry has freckles,
peppered like spice.

And Jerry has a pony
I rode on twice.

I think freckles
are *awfully* nice.

Aileen Fisher

MILLIONS OF PEOPLE

There are millions of people
In millions of places
And all of the people
Have different faces.
The tilt of the nose
May vary a bit;
The slant of the eye,
The curve of the lip.
You may look and look
At the fats and the thins
But no two are alike—
'Cept identical twins.
And they too may differ,
Even as we,
In some little way
That you cannot see.
No one can explain it
No one is to blame—
There are millions of people
And no two the same.

Jane W. Krows

WITH A FRIEND

I can talk with a friend
and walk with a friend
and share my umbrella
in the rain.

I can play with a friend
and stay with a friend
and learn with a friend
and explain.

I can eat with a friend
and compete with a friend
and even sometimes
disagree.

I can ride with a friend
and take pride with a friend.
A friend can mean
so much to me!

Vivian Gouled

DISCOVERY

In a puddle left from last week's rain,
    A friend of mine whose name is Joe
    Caught a tadpole, and showed me where
    Its froggy legs were beginning to grow.

Then we turned over a musty log,
    With lichens on it in a row,
    And found some fiddleheads of ferns
    Uncoiling out of the moss below.

We hunted around, and saw the first
Jack-in-the-pulpits beginning to show,
And even discovered under a rock
Where spotted salamanders go.

I learned all this one morning from Joe.
But how much more there is to know!

Harry Behn

I WONDER

I wonder how it would feel
If I
Could walk on the ceiling
Like a fly—
Or instead of sleeping
Stretched out flat
Slept upside down
Like a bat.
I wonder how I would look
If I
Had bright, colored wings
Like a butterfly—
Or instead of having
A short little nose,
Like an elephant's trunk,
Mine touched my toes.

Laura Arlon

DREAMS

Hold fast to dreams
For if dreams die
Life is a broken-winged bird
That cannot fly.

Hold fast to dreams
For when dreams go
Life is a barren field
Frozen with snow.

Langston Hughes

MY DREAM

I dreamed I sat down on the sky
And cut out stars all day;
Then scattered them at purple dusk
To light the Milky Way.

I dreamed the Old Man Moon came up
And whispered in my ear:
"You'll have to clear away those stars
When morning dawns, my dear!"

Annie Lee Funk

136

ONE DAY WHEN
WE WENT WALKING

One day when we went walking,
  I found a dragon's tooth,
  A dreadful dragon's tooth.
"A locust thorn," said Ruth.

One day when we went walking,
  I found a brownie's shoe,
  A brownie's button shoe.
"A dry pea pod," said Sue.

One day when we went walking,
  I found a mermaid's fan,
  A merry mermaid's fan.
"A scallop shell," said Dan.

One day when we went walking,
  I found a fairy's dress,
  A flannel fairy's dress.
"A mullein leaf," said Bess.

Next time that I go walking—
  Unless I meet an elf,
  A funny friendly elf—
  I'm going by myself!

Valine Hobbs

SEARCHING'S END

Adventure can be found
In many places,
In unfamiliar sounds,
Or in new faces.

Mary Pawlek

A FRIENDSHIP BRIDGE

I have a friend I've never seen;
  She lives in far Japan.
We write each other letters
  As often as we can.
It seems to me that letters
  Build a bridge across the sea
O'er which I go to visit her,
  And she comes to visit me!

Alice Crowell Hoffman

SECRET PLACE

Do you have a secret place
No one knows but you;
A quiet spot that's all your own?
I do!

My secret place is hidden
Beside a sparkling stream
Where tall oaks spread out friendly arms
And emerald fern fronds gleam.

In my secret place, I sit
And watch white clouds sail over;
Honeybees stop to sip
Sweet nectar from wild clover.

One day for my company
There came a dragonfly;
A turtle climbed upon a rock;
A silver snail trailed by.

We shared a common friendship,
But no one said a word.
The close-by murmur of the brook
Was the only sound heard.

As quietly as my guests came
The three left silently.
Something about each one of them
Promised secrecy.

O. J. Robertson

WONDERFUL WORLD

I can see
Trees and grass,
The sun and sky;

I can taste
Chocolate ice cream,
Apple pie;

I can hear
Music, laughter,
Words you said;

I can smell
Perfume, flowers,
Baking bread;

I can touch
Silk and velvet,
A baby's skin;

What a wonderful
World I'm in!

Eva Grant

THINGS TO TOUCH

Some things are so warm to touch,
  Like blankets in the sun,
Horses pulling heavy loads,
  A fresh-baked sugar bun.

Some things are so cool to touch,
  Like pebbles in a stream,
The marble on a table top,
  A dish of peach ice cream.

Some things are so smooth to touch,
  Like worn pews in a church,
Inside a mossy acorn cup,
  A bark-peeled stick of birch.

Some things are so soft to touch,
  Like snow, my cozy bed,
But best of all, my grandma's hand
  That gently strokes my head.

Camilla Walch Knox

THE PAINTING LESSON

Red and blue make purple
Yellow and blue make green.
Such a lot of colors
To paint a lovely scene.

Pink and blue make orchid;
Black and white make gray.
Now I'll dry my brushes
Until another day.

Frances Greenwood

KITCHEN SMELLS

I like the smells
The kitchen makes,
When my mother
Cooks and bakes.

Yummy rolls . . .
(I watch them rise)
Chocolate cakes,
Blueberry pies.

Broiled chickens,
Roasts a-roasting,
Crunchy cookies
Lightly toasting.

Jean Brabham McKinney

COLORS AND COLORS

Sometimes I think of colors
one by one by one . . .
  Pink for puffy evening clouds
  Yellow for the sun.

I think of watermelon
for something that is *green*,
  or an *orange* jack-o'-lantern
  on the night of Halloween.

I think of *purple* eggplant,
  and sky that's bright and *blue*,
  or *white* for sneaker laces,
  especially when they're new.

Sometimes I think of traffic lights
  when they just turn to *red*,
  or else I think how *black* it is
  at night when I'm in bed.

I might think of an elephant
  for something that is *gray*.
I like to think of colors
  and have some fun that way.

Vivian Gouled

THE MUSEUM DOOR

What's behind the museum door?
  Ancient necklaces,
  African art,
  The armor of knights,
  A peasant cart;

  Priceless old coins,
  A king's golden throne,
  Mummies in linen,
  And a dinosaur bone.

Lee Bennett Hopkins

THINGS TO DO
IF YOU ARE A SUBWAY

Pretend you are a dragon.
Live in underground caves.
Roar about underneath the city.
Swallow piles of people.
Spit them out at the next station.
Zoom through the darkness.
Go fast.
Make as much noise as you please.

Bobbi Katz

GOING UP!

First floor: "Linens, towels, mats!"
Second: "Ladies' dresses, hats!"
Third floor: "Furniture and rugs!"
Fourth: "Cosmetics, lotions, drugs!"
Fifth floor: "All out, girls and boys,
This floor—records, books, and toys!"

Eva Grant

CITY BLOCKADES

I feel so small
standing beneath the tall
buildings that wall
me and the pigeons in
from the light of the
sky.

Lee Bennett Hopkins

SUBWAY RUSH HOUR

Mingled
breath and smell
so close
mingled
black and white
so near
no room for fear.

Langston Hughes

CITY CHILD

The sidewalk is my yard,
  The lampost is my tree;
Up three long flights of stairs,
  My home is Flat 4 C.

The fire escape my porch,
  Where clothes hang out to dry;
All day the noise and rush,
  All night the trains go by.

Tall buildings all around
  Reach up and shadow me;
Sometimes the great big sun
  Comes peeping round to see.

All day the people pass,
  They hurry as they go;
But when they are my friends,
  They stop and say hello.

Lois Lenski

139

WAKE UP!

In the country
Everyone knows
It's morning when
The rooster crows.

But the city's
A different matter!
You're sure to hear
Garbage cans clatter,
Taxis toot,
Buses roar,
A paper slap
Against your door.

In country or city,
Morning sounds say,
"Wake up! Here comes
Another day."

Eva Grant

AN EXCITING TRIP

I ride the elevator up
    In our apartment house
And no one knows I'm playing
    For I'm quiet as any mouse.

But I pretend I'm piloting
    A rocket, swift as light,
That's full of passengers I'll land
    Upon the Moon tonight.

When we ride down, my rocket ship
    Falls like a shooting star,
And lands upon the Earth again
    Without the slightest jar.

The other people never know,
    As up and down we flip,
That I am taking them upon
    A wild, exciting trip!

Frances Gorman Risser

SPRING COMES TO THE CITY

Winter-shut windows are now agape,
Geraniums bloom on a fire escape,
A sidewalk is chalked with a hopscotch frame,
Boys in the street play a baseball game;
Girls jump rope to a chanting tune,
The ice-cream man will come out soon.
The scent of spring is in the air;
The signs of spring are everywhere.

Eva Grant

CITY CHILD'S THOUGHTS

Eggs come in cartons,
    Tomatoes in a box,
Carrots come in plastic crates,
    And honey comes in crocks.

Apples come in slatted crates,
    Each one tissue-wrapped.
Milk comes in a carton—
    Ice-cold and neatly capped.

But how they ever get inside
    The supermarket door
Is a mystery that puzzles me
    Each day a little more.

Ethel Jacobson

IS ONLY KNOWN

Rain in the city brings him out
Of sidewalk cracks. He crawls about,
Is very good at twists and bends;
But where he begins or where he ends
Or what his thoughts are, as he squirms,
Is only known to other worms.

Dorothy Aldis

FLOWER BOXES

Outside apartment windows,
On ledges row on row,
Are pretty flower boxes
Where fragrant blossoms grow,

Yellow jonquils nodding,
Violets, purple blue,
White narcissus, crocuses,
Crimson tulips, too.

Perched on window ledges
Around our tall high-rise,
Lovely rainbow gardens,
Blooming in the skies.

Jean Brabham McKinney

SKYSCRAPERS

The city's filled with fog today.
(They call it ''smog'' when it is gray
   and mixed with smoke.)
The buildings standing thin and tall
Don't scrape the smog away at all—
   Skyscrapers are a joke!

Rowena Bennett

CITY BEASTS

If I were in a jungle dark,
   I wouldn't cross a place
Where I might run into a lion
   Or tiger, face to face.

So in the city I will try
   To do the very same
For everybody knows that cars
   Are not exactly tame!

I'll wait at corners when I should,
   Watch where I go, and see
That I'm not crossing any trails
   Where city beasts might be.

Frances Gorman Risser

SIDEWALK BUILDERS

I like to watch the sidewalk crew
   Digging on our street.
Their drills and picks and shovels
   Drum a steady beat.

And when they've finished digging
   And the debris is cleared away,
Along come cement mixers,
   A new sidewalk to lay.

The soft cement flows out the chute
   In a smooth and creamy mound,
Like icing from a pastry tube.
   It makes a crunchy sound.

The cement is spread so carefully,
   Each corner must be square.
No bumps or lumps will they permit,
   Just smoothness everywhere.

They gaze upon their masterpiece,
   Then initial it with care,
So those who tread on it may know
   Whose artistry is there!

Lola Sneyd

A TIME FOR BUILDING

A dozen machines
come roaring down,
tractors and shovels,
hydraulics and dumps,
mixers and graders,
diggers and pumps,

pushing and groaning and moving the road
to another place in town.

Myra Cohn Livingston

THE CITY AND THE TRUCKS

The city sleeps in its unconcern, but the highways are awake
With searching flashes and grinding gears and the hiss of air in a brake;
When darkness comes, like a roll of drums three million engines roar
Under throbbing hoods, and the nation's goods are out on the roads once more.

The city wakens to meet old needs and perhaps some new desires,
And finds the answer to all it asks brought in on the rubber tires:
There is coal and milk, there is rope and silk, there is shelter and food and dress
That lumbered in when the dawn was thin on the night highway express.

The city moves in its ordered round and never asks or knows
How drivers inch through the murky night as the fog-bank comes and goes,
How they breast the beat of the blinding sleet and shift for the slippery climb,
How they stop a fire, or tinker a tire—and pull into town on time!

The city takes, and it goes its way, and the great dark hulks reload,
While mechanics grease, and test, and check, to make them safe for the road;
Then the crates are stacked and the boxes packed and the padding placed—and then
The tailboards slam, and the trailers ram—and the great trucks roll again!

Dorothy Brown Thompson

LAWN-MOWER

I'm the gardener today.
I push the lawn-mower
Across the grass.
  Zwuzz, wisssh, zwuzz, wisssh.

I'm the lawn's barber.
I'm cutting
Its green hair
  Short.

I push the lawn-mower
Across the grass.
  Zwuzz, wisssh.

Dorothy Baruch

MY PENCIL

A pencil is most marvelous.
It takes thoughts from out of us,
The things we've learned, our fancies free,
And puts them down where I can see.
And then in case they disappear
I know I'll find them somewhere near.

It draws me flowers, folks, and things,
Cars, houses, boats, and rocking swings.
And yet it cannot move itself
But simply loiters on a shelf,
Until some fingertips that know
Just pick it up and make it go.

Shirley R. Williams

MYSTERY OF THE TALKING FAN

Once there was a talking fan--
  Electrical his chatter.
I couldn't quite hear what he said
  And I hope it doesn't matter
Because one day somebody oiled
  His little whirling motor
And all the mystery was spoiled—
  He ran as still as water.

Maude Rubin

PAPER I

Paper is two kinds; to write on, to wrap with.
If you like to write, you write.
If you like to wrap, you wrap.
Some papers like writers, some like wrappers.
Are you a writer or a wrapper?

Carl Sandburg

FENCES

Fences
Make lines in fields
So cornstalks know
Where they live.
And so flowers
Can walk along
Beside them.

They are for
Roads to follow
So they can take
Cars where they want to go.

They keep horses and cows
From getting lost
And help them
Scratch their backs.

Fences are for boys and girls
To peek through,
Climb up,
Walk on,
And slide under.

They are for birds to sit on
When they talk together.

They have strong arms
To keep gardens, houses,
And playgrounds—safe.
They hold up bushes
And hold down ground.

Fences are good.

Deen McNeill

143

SONG OF BOXES

Oh, boxes and boxes and boxes
Are fun.
Boxes for rain and boxes
For sun.

Boxes for houses and boxes
For schools,
Boxes for working on
With my tools.

Cages for lions and big tiger cats,
Tables and chairs and special-day hats,
Bridges, tents, and space-monster men,
And boxes for putting boxes in.

Oh, boxes and boxes and boxes
Are fine.
If you don't have boxes,
Come play with mine.

Lillie D. Chaffin

TYPEWRITER SONG

Clickety-clack, clickety-clack!
The typewriter is typing a letter.
Clickety-clack over and back—
There's no way to write that is better.

Ring-a-ding, ring-a-ding dong!
The carriage goes back with a bang.
A ring and a dong is the typewriter's song—
A clickety, clack, and a clang.

Some typists are fast, some typists are slow;
There's a certain skill that it takes.
But no matter how slow at typing you go
You can't help but make some mistakes.

So, clickety-clack over and back
And a ring-a-ding and a dong
As you type away, day after day,
You are playing the typewriter song.

Jane W. Krows

A PICKLE JAR

A pickle jar
With a perforated lid
Makes a perfect place
For a captured katydid,
Or a bee with few belongings,
Or an avalanche of ants
Who are catering a dinner
Done of cookie crumbs on plants . . .
 Or a sluggish slug,
 A waylaid wasp,
 A mealyworm myopic,
Isn't it a captivating place
If you just don't drop it!

Constance Levy

THE MAILBOX

The mailbox on the corner
 Eats all the livelong day.
It nibbles cards and letters
 In an amazing way.
I wonder how it holds so much.
 If I ate pie and cake
The way that box eats letters,
 I'd have a stomachache!

Frances Gorman Risser

WATER IS A LOVELY THING

Water is a lovely thing—
Dark and ripply in a spring,
Dark and quiet in a pool,
In a puddle brown and cool;
In the river blue and gray,
In a raindrop silver gray,
In a fountain crystal bright;
In a pitcher frosty cold,
In a bubble pink and gold;
In a happy summer sea
Just as green as green can be;
In a rainbow far unfurled,
Every color in the world;
All the year from spring to spring,
Water is a lovely thing.

Julia W. Wolfe

MY GREAT BIG FLASHLIGHT

I had a great big flashlight
that went everywhere with me.
I used it all the long, long day
to see what I could see.

I took it in the closet
and closed the closet door;
I push aside my shoes and
sat down upon the floor.

I pointed my big flashlight
high up overhead—
just shirttails and pant cuffs—
so, I slid under the bed.

Lint, I found, a pair of socks;
and a bright red ball;
and lots of crazy bedsprings
but that was really all.

I took it into bed with me
and covered up my head.
Did I see something special there?
I saw wiggly toes instead!

I took it out into the yard
and turned it in the trees.
It didn't change a thing—
leaves were still green leaves!

I waved it at the mailman
and he waved back at me.
My flashlight didn't do a thing
as far as I could see.

And then at last I understood—
I really saw the light!
My flashlight was not a daytime thing.
It was made to shine at night!

Mary Ann Turner

THE ZIPPER

Zippers are a neat invention
With many uses I could mention,
Like zipping pillows in their slips
And zipping garment bags for trips.
Almost everything you wear
Has zippers hidden here and there.
How did we mortals manage clothes
Before someone invented those
Slipping, sliding zipper plaques
That fasten us and leave no gaps?
The only problem that I know
Is when the zipper will not go
Along its little metal track,
Both going up and coming back.
And if that zipper is a sticker
You'll have to be a zipper ripper.

Jane W. Krows

HINGES

A hinge is a handy thing to have
On a gate, a box, or a door.
You have them for fingers, toes, and knees.
Can you think of any more?

Hunt a few, stop and look—
A table leaf, chest top, and book.
And the casement window wide
That asks the summer wind inside.

The door of the stove, the freezer's too,
Must swing on hinges strong.
Your music-box cover goes up or down
On a hinge when you want a song.

A hinge can be made of many things
For hundreds of uses today.
In houses, cars, and school buildings
You'll find them all working away.

But nature designed the first hinge
Which people have copied so well.
And before giving hinges to you
God hinged the oyster's shell.

Edith Chapin Bowie

GRANDPA'S CLOCK

"Now, go to bed,"
Says Grandpa's clock.
"Tick-tock, tick-tock,
Tick-tock, tick-tock!"
So I put down my big red block,
And then pull off each wrinkled sock.

Alice F. Green

OUR WASHING MACHINE

Our washing machine went whisity whirr
Whisity whisity whisity whirr
One day at noon it went whisity click
Whisity whisity whisity click
Click grr click grr click grr click
   Call the repairman
   Fix it . . . Quick!

Patricia Hubbell

COVERS

Rugs cover floors,
Lids cover pots,
Leaves cover trees,
Roofs cover houses,
Shades cover lamps,
Socks cover feet,
Fur covers cats,
Grass covers yards,
Snow covers everything,
And covers cover me.

Dennis Kingsley

VACUUM CLEANER

The vacuum cleaner
Goes vvv,vvv,vvvv.
It vacuums the rugs,
The sofas and chairs,
Beneath the piano,
And up the stairs.
Vvv, vvv, vvvv,
Around the TV.
If I don't move
It might vacuum me!
Vvv, vvvv, vvvvv!

Ethel Jacobson

DRINKING FOUNTAIN

At first just a trickle,
Two drops splash and tickle.
And then there's a spurt,
A sudden big squirt,
Right smack in my eye:
The fountain must think
That I need a face-wash
More than a drink!

Ethel Jacobson

MY UMBRELLA

See this umbrella? It never got wet.
It never was out in a rainstorm yet.
When rain comes pouring from the sky,
My umbrella is home, all warm, all dry!
My umbrella has not caught a raindrop yet;
I am the one who always gets wet!

Gina Bell-Zano

WEARING GLASSES

Father wears glasses
   With rims of brown.
He wears them to work,
   He wears them to town.

Mother wears glasses
   With rims that glow.
She wears them to read,
   She wears them to sew.

And I wear glasses
   With rims that bend.
They don't have lenses—
   They're just pretend.

Leland B. Jacobs

STONE WALLS

I love to walk beside an old stone wall—
A wall meandering along the road,
Turning sometimes to wander through a field
Or skirt a thicket. A post-fence fairly marches,
But not my friendly wall. It seems content
To take its time, inviting me to rest
There on its comfortable, broad, gray back
And watch the antics of a lively squirrel.

Elizabeth Porter Kessler

PASSING BY THE JUNKYARD

Heaps of headlights
   stare
   at me.

Radiators, wheels
   and
   fan-belts
   smile.

And a thousand
   more parts—
   rusty and new,

Seem to say
   they'd all like
   to go
   on a
   car-ride
   again.

Charles J. Egita

DOORS

Big doors, little doors—
Every one fun!
Our home's front door
Is a great big one.

Car doors, store doors
Swinging out wide.
Our puppy's wee door
Lets him go outside.

The birdhouse door,
The cuckoo clock's,
The shiny door
On our new mailbox.

Pantry and oven doors,
Tidy and neat,
Opening to all sorts
Of goodies to eat.

Jean Brabham McKinney

SMOKE

A puff of blue smoke
Like a great big feather
Curls out of our chimney
In cold wintry weather—
A feather *some* giant
Might like to wear
Stuck up in his hat,
To town or the fair!

Ida Tyson Wagner

YELLOW HOUSE

The yellow house belongs to people now:
Curtains are crisply up, the sign is down.
I wonder if the owner knows his house
Once lived another life across the town?

And that, when it was sold, and must be moved,
It was so large, the workers sliced it through
As we might split an apple! Each half went
Its single journey, meeting here anew.

On stormy midnights, when the old boards creak,
Perhaps someone will guess, if he is keen,
That rooms are talking of the day they went
Outdoors for once—comparing what they've seen!

Lee Avery

THE TOASTER

A silver-scaled Dragon with jaws flaming red
Sits at my elbow and toasts my bread.
I hand him fat slices, and then, one by one,
He hands them back when he sees they are done.

William Jay Smith

FOOD'S FOUND

On vines
   Grapes and pumpkins
   grow on vines—
   thick as ropes—
   or on thin green lines
   as do squash
   and all of these:
   tomatoes, cucumbers,
   melons, and peas.
On trees
   Orchards offer
   all who come
   apple, cherry,
   peach and plum;
   grapefruit, orange,
   lemon, limes
   (these, of course,
   in tropic climes),
   apricot,
   and fig, and date—
   fruits we all
   appreciate.
   Nuts the nut trees
   will provide—
   even coconuts,
   round and wide.
   Hungry?
   Just look at the trees
   loaded down
   with delicacies!
Underground
   Carrots, potatoes,
   and turnips grow
   deep under the ground—
   though green leaves show—
   parsnips,
   and onions. But
   you think to look
   the peanut?

Elsie S. Lindgren

MORNING TOAST

My toast has such a nice crunchable
   sound
As I bite my piece that's all buttered
   and browned.
Though my egg is pure silver and
   gold in my dish,
And my orange and cocoa quite all
   one could wish
Still, I know that at breakfast the
   thing I like most
Is my buttered, brown, munchable,
   crunchable toast!

Doris I. Bateman

CELERY

Celery, raw,
Develops the jaw,
But celery, stewed,
Is more quietly chewed.

Ogden Nash

TUG-OF-WAR

I marvel at all
The power I need
When I brace myself
To pull up a weed.

It isn't the distance
The roots extend—
The world is attached
To the other end!

May Richstone

MY DRUM

Tap . . .
Tap . . .
Tap, tap, tap . . .
Tap . . .
Tap . . .
Tap, tap, tap.

Hear the drum . . .
Hear the drum . . .
Hear the drum, drum, drum
Hear the drum.

See the drum . . .
See the drum . . .
See the drum, drum, drum
See the drum.

It's a fine new drum
And I beat this drum
With the sticks . . .
With the sticks . . .

And I tap, tap, tap
And I tap, tap, tap
On my drum . . .
On my drum.

Rat-a-tat tat,
Rat-a-tat tat,
Rat-a-tat,
Rat-a-tat,
Tat, tat, tat.

And I beat, beat, beat
And I beat, beat, beat,
On my drum . . .
On my drum.

And I tap, tap, tap
And I tap, tap, tap
With the sticks . . .
With the sticks . . .

Tap . . .
Tap . . .
Tap, tap, tap . . .
Tap . . .
Tap . . .
Tap, tap, tap.

Hear the drum . . .
Hear the drum . . .
Hear the drum, drum, drum
Hear the drum.

My drum . . .
My drum . . .
I tap, tap, tap
On my drum.

My drum . . .
My drum.

Dorothy Z. Seymour

LEWIS HAS A TRUMPET

A trumpet
A trumpet
Lewis has a trumpet
A bright one that's yellow
A loud proud horn.
He blows it in the evening
When the moon is newly rising
He blows it when it's raining
In the cold and misty morn
It honks and it whistles
It roars like a lion
It rumbles like a lion
With a wheezy huffing hum
His parents say it's awful
Oh really simply awful
But
Lewis says he loves it
It's such a handsome trumpet
And when he's through with trumpets
He's going to buy a drum.

Karla Kuskin

PREFERRED VEHICLES

A bicycle's fine for a little trip
    Up the street or down;
An automobile for a longer trip,
    Off to another town;
An airplane's fine for around the world,
    To many a far-out place;
And a rocket, oh, for the longest trip
    Away into outer space.

Leland B. Jacobs

NAUGHTY DONNA

I like getting toys that will
make lots of noise—
Especially the kind
That will scare all the boys!

Lee Bennett Hopkins

149

FERRYBOATS

Over the river,
Over the bay,
Ferryboats travel
Every day.

Most of the people
Crowd to the side
Just to enjoy
Their ferryboat ride.

Watching the seagulls,
Laughing with friends,
I'm always sorry
When the ride ends.

James S. Tippett

MY BIKE

I'm off like lightning! Watch me go
  Up the hill, pumping slow,
Then zooming down the other side
  Like a roller-coaster ride.

Through the puddles
  My bike is a boat;
My wet wheels keep
  Me dry while I float.

The sidewalk's my highway
  As I whizz along,
Singing a happy
  Pedaling song.

Bobbe Indgin

THE WHEEL

How very strangely we should feel
If someone had not made a wheel!
No wagon would have crossed the plain,
No puffing engine, no speeding train.

No cart or carriage would there be,
Or roller skates for you and me,
No bicycle or automobile,
If someone had not made a wheel.

Josephine Van Dolzen Pease

THERE ARE SO MANY WAYS OF GOING PLACES

Big yellow trolley lumbers along,
Long black subway sings an under song,
Airplanes swoop and flash in the sky,
Noisy old elevated goes rocketing by.
Boats across the water—back and forth they go,
Big boats and little boats, fast boats and slow.
Trains puff and thunder; their engines have a headlight;
They have a special kind of car where you can sleep all night.
Tall fat buses on the Avenue,
They will stop for anyone—even—just—you.
All kinds of autos rush down the street.
And then there are always—your own two feet.

Leslie Thompson

THE SUBWAY TRAIN

The subway train, the subway train,
If you'll permit me to explain,
Is like a busy beetle black
That scoots along the silver track.
And, whether it be night or day,
The beetle has to light its way,
Because the only place it's found
Is deep, deep, deep, deep, underground.

Leland B. Jacobs

THE WISE TRAIN

The train went rushing far away,
  But left the track behind it,
So when it took the road again,
  'Twould know the way to find it!

J. Lilian Vandevere

ENGINE

Work, little engine,
  Pull us along;
Puff, little engine,
  Puff a gay song!

Work, little engine,
  Pull, pull, pull!
Draw forth cars
  That are full, full, full!

Work, little engine,
  Blizzard or rain;
Puff, little engine,
  Pull the long train!

Nona Keen Duffy

NIGHT TRUCKS

They tunnel through darkness,
  Their eyes on the ground.
They flay at the night with
  Their paddles of sound.

They roar and they rumble.
  They screech and they brake.
They sew up the gaps
  That far distances make.

Thelma Ireland

WHEN WE DRIVE THROUGH A TUNNEL

Whenever we drive through a tunnel
  My dad always blows the horn.
Mom tells him not to be childish,
  But Dad just smiles at her scorn.

Dad knows that I love that mournful sound—
Echoing, echoing all around
In a hollow boat-whistle sort of way,
Sad and drawn-out across the bay.

It gives me a feeling I just can't explain —
A kind of lonesomeness, almost a pain,
As, just for a second, the world seems to change
And everything looks to be different and strange.

And I am strange, too—someone old, sad, and wise—
but the sound fades away, and that odd feeling dies.
Then I'm glad to be me again, riding along
With my dad at the wheel and Mom humming a song.

But I know when I'm grown up and married,
  And after my children are born,
Whenever we drive through a tunnel
  They'll want me to blow my horn.

Virginia S. Baldridge

MAGIC OLD AND NEW

People in stories took magical flights—
The carpet that flapped through Arabian Nights,
The little lame prince with his traveling cloak
The witches on broomsticks, and ghosts in the smoke;
Peter Pan's fairy dust blown on the shoulder
Performed very well if one didn't grow older;
And silver shoes worked to bring Dorothy back
From the Land of Oz.
　　　But today you can pack,
And buy a jet-ticket, and climb a short stair,
And fasten a seat belt, and—whoosh—through the air,
And before you can finish your lunch, you are there!

Dorothy Brown Thompson

JET PLANE

A ghostly herd comes thundering—
Crash! A barrier's downed:
And airy plains reecho
With wild stampedes of sound.

Then, suddenly, a silence!
No sign of what zoomed by
Except a widening trail of dust
Across the prairie sky.

Alice Briley

SATELLITE

I am a little satellite;
I sparkle with a yellow light.
I orbit round the earth, and then
I speed around and back again.
Beep, beep!
Swish, swish, swish!
Beep, beep!
Swish, swish, swish!
Beep, beep!

Ollie James Robertson

FLYING

In early days,
　A joyous sight,
High and higher,
　Flew the kite.

And next was seen,
　So free and fair,
The round balloon
　Upon the air.

But now like mighty birds
　That fly,
The winged airplane
　Soars the sky!

Josephine Van Dolzen Pease

NEW PET

We've something new at our house now,
   A something soft and small.
But though it cries and wiggles so,
   It's not a pig at all!

It drinks just milk and gulps it down
   Till it looks very fat.
It can't chase mice; do you know why?
   It isn't any cat!

It cries at night; I guess that's 'cause
   It's lonely for its mother.
No, it's not a puppy dog.
   It's a baby brother!

Lois F. Pasley

LICKETY SPLIT

Kitten love
Is often sticky:
Busy tongue
Can be too "icky."

Dick Hayman

BIRD IN THE HAND

I clean the cage, replenish seeds,
Change the water, watch her needs,
In fact, obey the slightest tweet
From one imperious parakeet!

On a branch outside, the wild birds sway,
And sing to me the livelong day;
That proverb's fine, but by some quirk,
The bird in the hand's a lot more work!

Lee Avery

SELF-STARTING

Some of my toys you must wind with a key.
Some of them pull with a string.
Some are what Daddy calls "battery run"
When you just push a lever-like thing.
But my really true kitten goes all by herself,
And I notice whenever I'm near,
She has a small motor inside of her skin,
One that you really can hear.

Margaret Hillert

CHINESE PROVERB

A lame cat
is better than a swift horse
when rats infest
the palace.

Anonymous

153

OSCAR

Oscar is a little pup,
A downy, browny, little pup,
A plumpy, lumpy, little pup,
Who ran away one day.

He trotted down a busy street,
A hooty, tooty, busy street,
A whizzy, dizzy, busy street,
And ran away one day.

He sniffed at a butcher store,
He scratched at a bakery door,
He tracked up a fresh-waxed floor
As he ran away one day.

Now Oscar wears a little leash,
A longish, little, leather leash,
A pull-and-tug-it leather leash,
Every, every day.

Oscar is a little pup,
A yippy, yappy, little pup,
A sniffy, scratchy, little pup,
Who stays at home all day.

Lillie D. Chaffin

MY DOG

His feet are big,
His ears are floppy.
When he eats
He's very sloppy.
He can't do tricks—
Jump over sticks
Or anything that's clever.
But he's my own,
My very own,
And I'll love him
Forever!

Helen Lorraine

THE LIGHTHOUSE LABRADOR

In a lighthouse off the bay
    lives a labrador named Shay
Shay has nothing to do all day
    but sit and watch the sea lions play.
Once in a while he goes ashore,
    but says Shay, the lighthouse labrador,
"City life is such a bore—
rushing, pushing, such a rat race.
I prefer a slower pace;
a quiet place,
where all I hear
are seagulls screeching in my ear
and foghorns blowing all the night.
Maybe for you this isn't right,
but this is where I want to be
because city life is not for me."

Wendy Mary Cruse

OUR LITTLE BLACK DOG

Our little black dog barks at each tiny thing—
A fly on a fence or a bird on the wing,
A leaf on a tree or a kite in the sky,
A rumpled-up newspaper scurrying by.
She grumbles at gravel and pebbles and stones;
She bellows at branches and dirty old bones;
She trumpets at insects—a beetle or bee.
But—bark at a stranger? No, not she!

We wanted a watchdog, and that's what we got—
Except that she watches the things she should not!
Good leather shoes that are easy to chew,
Soft comfy cushions, so fluffy and new.
She watches for letters and papers and books;
She watches for food scraps each time Mother cooks;
She watches for offers to sit on a knee.
But—watch for a stranger? No, not she!

Daphne Doward

CONVERSATION

Cackle, gobble, quack, and crow,
Neigh and bray and bleat and low,
Twitter, chirrup, cheep, and coo,
Bark and growl and purr and mew.

Humming, buzzing, hiss, and sting,
Hoot and cuckoo, caw and sing,
Squeal and grunt and snort and squawk;
Who said, "Only people talk"?

Aletha M. Bonner

KANGAROO RIDE

I suppose it would be rather
    A risky thing to do,
But I'd like to go out riding
    On a leaping kangaroo!

I expect it would be bumpy
    Each time he touched the ground,
And hard to keep from slipping,
    With every lengthy bound;

But I shouldn't mind the jolting,
    Or having people stare,
With Australian towns behind me,
    And cool wind in my hair!

Elaine V. Emans

SCHOOL OF MINNOWS

Down in the brook where the water runs cool—
That's where the minnows are going to school!
What do they study, I wonder, and then,
When do they get to go home again?

Schools for the fish aren't like mine, I guess—
No teachers or blackboards or books—just recess!
When Daddy says, "Look! School of minnows there, Son!"
It sure looks to me like they're just having fun!

Jane Keefer Frey

A HOUSE FOR ONE

The turtle children,
Sister and brother,
Do not live in one house
With their father and mother.
Each baby turtle
Is happy alone
In a snug little house
Of his very own.

Laura Arlon

LITTLE BUNNY RABBITS

Oh, little bunny rabbits
    With funny little tails,
And ears so long you seem to me
    Like boats with furry sails,

You nibble at your cabbages;
    Your ears go flippy-flop.
Then all at once, you turn away,
    And hop and hop and hop!

Frances Arnold Greenwood

THE SEAL

I could squeal
about the seal.
He's sleek and swift and wet.
He can balance a ball—
If it doesn't fall!
And sing—if he doesn't forget!

He's soft to feel
The lovely seal,
And just as black as jet.
His favorite dish
Is a wiggly fish.
Oh, what a charming pet!

Claire Boiko

QUESTION

A baby pig
Has a squeal quite big,
A kitten can mew,
An owlet hoo,
But how does a llama
Call his mama?

Margaret E. Singleton

IF YOU SHOULD MEET A CROCODILE

If you should meet a Crocodile
Don't take a stick and poke him;
Ignore the welcome in his smile,
Be careful not to stroke him.
For as he sleeps upon the Nile,
He thinner gets and thinner;
And whene'er you meet a Crocodile
He's ready for his dinner.

Unknown

RHINO

The rhino wears a prominent horn
And relishes dry shrub and thorn.
He has a prehistoric savor,
Prehensile mouth and unreal flavor.
His only friend, the tickbird, picks
His rough thick hide for burrs and ticks.
Though rhinos do not look too well
I hear they run like the gazelle,
Courageously they charge a train
And neither is the same again.
Irascible and very snappy,
Mudwallows make them faintly happy.
I would love to watch a herd,
Each rhino with his little bird.

Katherine Saunders

156

SLEEPY OYSTER

The storm is raging up above,
   And waves are dashing high,
The sea birds, screaming, fly to land,
   As thunder rocks the sky.

But down below in waters calm
   The oyster sleeps away;
Quite heedless of the wind and waves,
   He snoozes, night and day.

He does not shout and rant and rave,
   Nor bolts of lightning hurl,
He's dozing in the oyster bed,
   And dreaming up a pearl!

Frances Gorman Risser

THE SILENT ONE

He never makes a sound
To tell when he's around;
Can't sing when he feels sunny
Or laugh when something's funny;
Although he may not mind
Being the silent kind,
I wish that a giraffe
Could laugh.

Margaret E. Singleton

NECKS

The swan has a neck that is curly and long.
The camel has one that is shaggy and strong.
But the spotted giraffe
Has a neck and a half.

Rowena Bennett

COYOTE

   With furtive eyes
he slinks from rim to rim;
rhythm of jackrabbit hop;
scratching of desert sparrow
quickens his hunger.
   In the moon's cold light,
savage with longing,
he lifts his muzzle to stars.
   Cliffs echo and reecho,
bounce back
long eerie wails.

Gertrude May Lutz

THE HIPPOPOTAMUS

In the squdgy river,
   Down the oozely bank,
Where the ripples shiver
   And the reeds are rank,

Where the purple Kippo
   Makes an awful fuss,
Lives the hip-hip-hippo,
   Hippo-pot-a-mus!

You would think him dreaming
   Where the mud is deep.
It is only seeming—
   He is not asleep.

Better not disturb him—
   There'd be an awful fuss
If you touched the Hippo
   Hippo-pot-a-mus.

Georgia Roberts Durston

157

BIRD CARPENTER

Carpenters use nails and hammers,
　Planes and levels,
　Saws and rules.

Birds build houses so much simpler—
　Beaks are all
　They have for tools.

Leland B. Jacobs

THE POLLYWOG

A fat pollywog
　In a pool in the bog
　　Began to feel frightfully queer.
His body felt strange,
　But he didn't have pains,
　　He only felt solemn and drear.

His rusty black coat
　Got white at the throat
　　And speckled with green on the back.
His tail shrank and shrank,
　Then he crawled on the bank
　　And found that he made a queer track.

There were four legs so neat
　With lovely webbed feet
　　Grown right to that fat pollywog.
And the first time he spoke
　He cried with a croak,
　　"Mercy me, I've turned into a frog!"

Shirley R. Williams

SPRING SILHOUETTE

Breathless under cloudless sky
Seeing eagle soar and fly—
　Wondering just how.

Heartbeats keeping pace with him
As the cliffs he dares to skim;
Even sunlight would seem dim—
　If I, too, knew how.

Seeing great bird diving down
Toward its nest a sculptured crown
On the cliff's sheer brow;
Soon I must return to town—
　Wing king, show me how!

Don Marshall

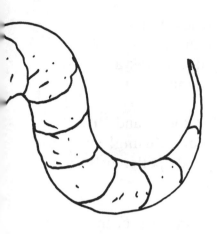

SUMMER

Little green lizard, sitting on a stone,
Little blond boy, watching all alone.
Quick green movement, almost like a rocket;
Little boy is quicker—lizard's in his pocket.

Caryl M. Kerber

BE LIKE THE BIRD

Be like the bird, who
Halting in his flight
On limb too slight
Feels it give way beneath him,
Yet sings
Knowing that he hath wings.

Victor Hugo

GARDEN SNAKE

I saw a snake and ran away . . .
Some snakes are dangerous, they say;
But mother says that kind is good,
And eats up insects for his food.

So when he wiggles in the grass
I'll stand aside and watch him pass,
And tell myself, "There's no mistake,
It's just a harmless garden snake!"

Muriel L. Sonne

BIRD WALK

Jimmy Sparrow, as I pass,
Goes a-hopping on the grass,
Just as though he had some things
Up inside like little springs.
So he doesn't walk at all,
Just goes bouncing like a ball.
Hippity-hop he goes, then stops.
    Hippity-hop,
        Hop-hop,
            Hop, hop!

Peter Pigeon, while he walks,
Talks his little cooing talks,
Pumping with his head as though
That's what makes his two feet go.
Round the fountain, round and round
Just as though he had been wound,
Pumpity-pump, and then a jump.
    Pumpity-pump,
        Pump-pump,
            Pump, pump!

Shirley R. Williams

BIRD ON MY FIRE ESCAPE

You could have built
    Your children's nest
In a lofty tree,
    Like all the rest.

But you chose a most
    Unlikely spot,
Where the wind blows cold,
    And the sun shines hot.

Did you settle near me
    Just so I
Could help you watch
    Your fledglings fly?

Eva Grant

ABOUT WORDS

Words are little singing sounds
for saying over and over.
They run in little bootstep tracks
on pages, cover to cover.
They make us bridges and trees and pigs
and a house for a little red hen.
They let us see things all over the world
without even pictures of them.

Sometimes they look almost the same,
like children in a line.
Sometimes they're not like they look at all.
And some of the time they rhyme—
like coat and boat
and sing and swing,
and cones and bones and phones.
Sometimes they just go splashing along
like water over stones.

Words can take us for long, long rides
on planes
or trains,
or the bus.
Words are very wonderful things
because they talk to us.

Gertrude L. Robb

SPELLING BEE

It takes a good speller
to spell *cellar*,
separate, and *benefiting*;
not omitting
cemetery, *cataclysm*,
picnicker and *pessimism*.
And have you ever tried
innocuous, *inoculate*,
dessert, *deserted*, *desiccate*;
divide and *spied*,
gnat, *knickers*, *gnome*,
crumb, *crypt*, and *chrome*;
surreptitious, *supersede*,
delete, *dilate*, *impede*?

David McCord

WORDS

Words are the oddest things
    Haven't you found?
Sometimes they don't look a
    Bit like they sound.

There are "to," "too," and "two."
    Watch which you're using!
If you're not a good speller, it's
    Very confusing.

Sometimes one word can mean
    Different things;
We draw with straight "rulers"
    Or else it means "kings."

When you recite "bow,"
    But shoot with a "bow."
Words are the oddest things!
    Don't you think so?

Nelle Arnold

SEE HOW THEY RUN!

Run is a word with meanings galore.
I'll think of some. You think of more.
Run is a break in your mother's hose;
Run is what paint does all over your clothes.
You run for the bus and for office, too;
Prices run high, but that's nothing new.
You run up a seam, run before you jump,
Run onto a bargain, and over a bump.
Peaches run fine and big this season;
Sailboats run with the wind with reason.
A run in baseball can win the game;
A horse run too hard will often go lame.
And on we could run for many a day
Compounding nouns—rundown, runaway,
Runoff, run-in, run-out, runabout.
Please! Please! No need to shout,
For I've run down! But it's been fun
Naming ways to use the word **run**.

Grace Mayr

A PICKLE IS LONG

A pickle is long
And an orange is round,
But I wonder sometimes . . .
Is there shape to a sound
   like a whisper
      or a whistle
         or a laugh
            or a sneeze?
What shapes would you think of
   for sounds like these?

Vivian Gouled

WORDS

Words are wonderful.
Words are weird:
  wanton, wicked,
  writhing, witless,
  wrathful, winsome,
  whooping, whispering,
  woebegone, withering,
  warping, weakening,
  wanting, wresting,
  worrisome, wincing,
  wishful, winning.
Words are weird.
Words are wonderful.

Veronica Keillor

WORDS

I like stand-up words.
  straight   still
I like sit-down words.
  slide   spill
I like scary words.
  Whooo's there?
I like noisy words.
  Bang!   Blare!
I like happy words.
  grin   giggle
I like funny words.
  hoot   wiggle
I like sleepy words.
  soft pillow
I like sad words.
  weeping willow
I like pretty words.
  tinkle   silk
I like eating words.
  bread   milk

Glenda Greve

I LOVE WORDS

Rhyming words;
Singing birds,
Soft blue sky,
Lullaby,
Lion's roar,
Cellar door,
Blinking,
Winking,
Twinkling,
Sprinkling,
Dance with glee,
Melody,
Spun and sun!
Rhyming's fun.

Eva Grant

161

THE DICTIONARY

I hope that I shall never be
Devoid of curiosity
About the meaning of a word
Which I have either seen or heard.

I hope when of a word I'm wary
I'll always seek a dictionary,
And learn to use it as a friend
For help and counsel without end.

Genieve P. Brunkow

DICTIONARY

A Dictionary's where you can look things up
    To see if they're really there:
        To see if what you breathe is AIR,
        If what you sit on is a CHAIR,
        If what you comb is curly HAIR,
        If what you drink is from a CUP.
A Dictionary's where you can look things up
    To see if they're really there.

William Jay Smith

THE ALPHABET

The alphabet starts
With ABC.
It always ends
With XYZ,
And in between,
All set in a row,
Are twenty other
Letters to know.
It's a long, long, way,
As you can see,
From ABC
To XYZ.

Leland B. Jacobs

MY WORD!

A noun is quite dependable;
It never leaves you in suspense!
But a participle may be dangling,
And a verb is always tense!

W. Lowrie Kay

ZOONS

Zinkety-zankety-zoons,
It's fun to find words
That rhyme with *zoons*—
Cartoons, buffoons,
Balloons, and tunes.
Some animal words
Rhyme with *zoons*—
Raccoons and loons,
Cocoons, baboons.
Yes, many words
Rhyme with *zoons*—
You can use prunes,
Or moons, or spoons.
And then you're not done;
You've just begun
Finding words
To rhyme with *zoons*—
Zinkety-zankety,
Zinkety-zankety,
Zinkety-zankety-zoons.

Florence E. Sullivan

STAND-INS

Pronouns are our stand-in words;
They play the part of nouns—
Proper ones like Bill or Jim,
And common ones like town.

He is one, and him and it—
They fit in anywhere
And do their work so quietly
We hardly know they're there.

Evantha Caldwell

THINK OF IT

"Go quickly," says my mother
or some other
hurry person.
    Then I think of fast things—
       hummingbird wings
       lizards darting
       racers starting
       bicycle wheels
       automobiles
       wind through the trees
       some angry bees—
       and I'm quick!

"Sh-h-h!" says my mother
or some other
tiptoe person.
    Then I think of still things—
       empty swings
       dark nights
       soaring kites
       thick, soft mittens
       newborn kittens
       whispered prayers
       sleeping bears—
       and I'm quiet!

"Slow down," says my mother
or some other
getting tired person.
    Then I think of lazy things—
       yawning kings
       elephants strolling
       plump pigs rolling
       a cow chewing cud
       some oozing mud
       inchworm on my hand
       sifting sand—
and I go slow!

Bette Killion

A CLICHÉ

A cliché
is what we all say
when we're too lazy
to find another way

and so we say

warm as toast,
quiet as a mouse,
slow as molasses,
quick as a wink.

Think,
Is toast the warmest thing you know?
Think again, it might not be so.
Think again: it might even be snow!
Soft as lamb's wool, fleecy snow,
a lacy shawl of new-fallen snow.

Listen to that mouse go
scuttling and clawing,
nibbling and pawing.
A mouse can speak
if only a squeak.

Is a mouse the quietest thing you know?
Think again, it might not be so.
Think again: it might be a shadow.
Quiet as a shadow,
quiet as growing grass,
quiet as a pillow,
or a looking glass.

Slow as molasses,
quick as a wink.
Before you say so,
take time to think.

Eve Merriam

163

THE REMINDER

Where storm had churned the garden earth, we knelt
To firm the roots, and felt a sting of stone—
An arrowhead—there where the tall corn grew.

Precisely chipped and luminous it shone,
Springwater cool against the open palm,
All roughness smoothed by time and fingers dust
How many years? And where our red brick house
Now stands, whose teepee stood? And is this gust
The wind, or brushwood smoke that tears the eye?

We listen and the corn stands listening, too.
How many deer received this stone and heard
This sound, so like the pad of buckskin shoe?
Through all the years, erased by winds and rains,
So much has passed. An arrowhead remains.

Bessie F. Collins

CANDLE MAKING

Dip the wick into the tallow,
Melted hot and golden yellow.
Watch it grow,
Watch it grow,
Like a rolling ball of snow.

In and out and in again,
Dip and dip and dip, and then,
Round and smooth
And candle-thick,
Put it in the candlestick.

Through the darkness
Of the night,
It will make
A lovely light.

J. Van Dolzen Pease

THE COVERED WAGON

When our forefathers
With courage true
Left the old home
For the new,

'Neath starry sky
And blazing sun
The covered wagon
Was their home.

Sheltering them
By night and day,
Bearing them safely
On their way,

Carrying in
Its circling fold
The homely comforts
Loved of old,

Faithful
Till the journey's end,
The covered wagon
Was their friend.

J. Van Dolzen Pease

THE STAGECOACH

Down the valley and over the hill,
With whirling wheels and hoofbeats drumming,
Near and nearer and nearer still,
The stagecoach is coming! The stagecoach is coming!

High on his seat see the driver ride!
He cracks his whip and calls aloud.
The people run from every side,
A welcoming and joyful crowd.

Bag and baggage piled on high
Sway against the setting sun!
Like clouds across the wind-blown sky,
The dashing horses onward run!

With beating hearts and happy smiles,
Proudly the travelers sit within,
How wonderfully swift the journeying miles!
How wondrously sweet the welcoming din!

Down the valley and over the hill,
With whirling wheels and hoofbeats drumming,
Near and nearer and nearer still,
The stagecoach is coming! The stagecoach is coming!

Josephine Van Dolzen Pease

HOME OF YESTERDAY

A little log cabin rests on our land.
Its walls a-crumble—it can barely stand,
Its one lone room is a sight to see—
A sight from another century.
For a table, a box with tree-limb legs,
For chairs, some old-time cracker kegs,
And on the floor no fancy mat—
Just plain earth trodden down flat.
A small fireplace—the cooking spot,
And source of what light the family got.
I'd like to go back through the years
And share the joys, the trials, the fears
Of those brave souls who came this way
To build the cabin I'm viewing today.

William Hurley

FRONTIERS

Some people say there are no frontiers
Awaiting youth today;
That the chances our forefathers had
With time have passed away.
There are no new lands spread afar
Where the bold in heart may go.
That may be true, but think a while—
There are *new* frontiers, we know!

How many paths may still be left
In earth and air and sea,
Each with a call to the pioneer,
"Oh, come and follow me!"
Who knows the course or has a chart
Where the mind of man may seek
Some knowledge new, some wisdom true?
Of these frontiers I speak.

Oh, youth, the challenge is flung to you,
Your new frontiers to find.
There is no future bleak and bare
To an eager and earnest mind.
So bravely seek the hidden goals
And face each new frontier
With a conquering eye, with courage high,
And the heart of a pioneer!

M. Lucille Ford

MEHITABLE

Great-Grandmother's doll, Mehitable,
  In her quaint old-fashioned gown,
Is dressed exactly the way she was
  When she came from London town.
She wears a bonnet and cloak of gray,
  And looks like a Quaker maid;
She thinks the dolls in their Paris gowns
  Quite worldly, I am afraid.

I always feel that she's very wise—
  She has lived so long, you see.
If she could speak, I am very sure,
  She would tell strange tales to me.
I take great care of Mehitable,
  In her quaint old-fashioned gown,
Great-Grandmother's doll of long ago,
  Whose home was in Boston town.

Winifred C. Marshall

LONG, LONG AGO

Did you ever stop to think
That long, long ago,
There were no motor cars
Passing in a row!

There were no trains
On long, shining tracks,
No mighty steamboats
With tall smokestacks!

No mail man stopping
At every door,
No truck with packages
Bought at the store!

Who were the bearers
Of burdens then?
The sturdy backs
Of brave, strong men!

J. Van Dolzen Pease

MAKING MAPS

I love to make maps!
I think it's great fun—
Making the boundaries,
And then, one by one,
Putting in railroads,
And each river bend,
And the tiny towns
Where little roads end.
I draw in mountains,
And often a lake,
And I've even had
Long bridges to make!
I like to do highways,
And when they are drawn
I dream that they take me
Where I've never gone.

Elaine V. Emans

GEOGRAPHY

I think geography is *fun!*
  Upon the map, with care,
I trace strange countries, one by one,
  And travel ev'rywhere!

I seek out cities far away,
  Follow down rivers blue,
Trace here a lake, and there a bay,
  Whose names to me are new!

I visit China and Japan;
  I journey down the Rhine!
Then, trav'ling with a caravan,
  A "desert ship" is mine;

I wander in far Timbuctoo;
  In India's plains I trek!
The vales of Greece I wander through,
  And Brazil's rivers check!

To all these places on the map
  I travel, and with ease!
An open book upon my lap,
  I sail the seven seas!

Clarence Mansfield Lindsay

MAPS

I like to study foreign maps;
Some time I'll take a trip, perhaps,

I'd like to hop upon a plane,
And fly to distant, sunny Spain.

I'd like to see the River Nile,
And linger there a little while.

I'd like to see the London Tower
This very month, and day, and hour.

But if I cannot go today,
I'll play that I am going away.

I like to study foreign maps;
Some time I'll go away, perhaps.

Edith Amelia Skiles

FRIENDS AROUND THE WORLD

If I should go to London
  I'd find a child like me;
He'd probably play cricket
  And have bread and jam for tea.

If I should go to Holland
  When winter's on the sea,
I'd find the children skating
  Upon the Zuyder Zee.

If I should go to China,
  Or down to Mexico
I'd find kites or balls or marbles
  Or something I would know.

It's curious to think of it—
  Wherever I might be,
In Spain or France or Russia,
  I'd find children just like me.

Blanche Jennings Thompson

A SAFE DRIVER

I never worry when my dad
Is in the driver's seat,
For he drives very carefully
Along the busy street.

He never fails to signal
When turning left or right;
And now he stops the car, because
He's come to a red light.

When he is driving by a school,
He always drives quite slow;
The long, long list of traffic laws
He always seems to know.

Someday, I'll drive like Daddy,
Like him, go everywhere,
And I'll never get a ticket
'Cause I'll always drive with care.

Jacqueline Rowland

TRAFFIC LIGHTS

Red light, red light,
What do you say?
I say, "Stop,
And stop right away!"

Yellow light, yellow light,
What do you mean?
I mean "Wait—
Till the light turns green!"

Green light, green light,
What do you say?
I say, "Cross!
First look each way!"

Thank, thank you,
Red, yellow, green;
Now I know
What traffic lights mean!

Vivian Gouled

CROSSING THE STREET

Traffic lights are meant to be
Safety lights for you and me:
    Green means GO!
        First look each way!
    Yellow—WAIT!
        A slight delay!
    Red means STOP!
        And stop right then
        until it's green,
        then go again!
So every time we cross the street
Let's watch the lights and tell our feet!

Vivian G. Gouled

SAFETY TIPS

When you do your dishes
Or bake your pies and bread—
Be sure to close the cupboard doors
Or you may bump your head!

"Oh, Polly, put the kettles on!"
But turn the handles *in,*
For if you hit them they may spill
And the mess will be a sin.

To carry matches in the car,
Or on a camping trip,
Take them in a metal box—
A no-fire safety tip!

Wastebaskets are for papers
And lint and dirt and trash.
Be sure you dunk the lighted match
And dampen ash-tray ash.

In dishpan and in cupboard drawers
Give sharp knives special care.
Wall holders are the place to keep
Them safe for longer wear.

Don't park your skates on cellar steps
Or toys upon the stairs.
You *could* fall down and break your bones
In ones or threes or pairs.

Gladys I. Hamilton

THE DARK

The dark is warm
As the touch of fur.
The dark is soft
As a kitten's purr.
It wraps me snug
In velvet wings
With comfortable
Murmurings.

The dark says, "Sleep,
My small one, rest
Like a baby wren
In its tree-house nest."
It watches me
With loving looks
And brings me dreams
Like storybooks.

Ethel Jacobson

SLEEPING SILENT

Crowds of night-cloud
hang suspended
mid star
and stir
of leafless tree.

Their sleeping-silent
midnight-magic
calls to me.

Barbara M. Hales

THE NIGHT SKY

When at night I've gone to bed,
With stars a-twinkling overhead,
Lots of things I think about
As I watch them peeping out.

Do the smallest stars all play
Out there on the Milky Way?
When they're thirsty do you think
From the Dipper they might drink?

Are the little stars up there
Frightened when they see the Bear?
I am sure he wouldn't bite,

For I watch him every night,
And his picture in my book
Has a kind and friendly look.

Lots of others are up there
Far above me in the air.
Sometimes I can find the Lion
And the Dog of good Orion.

It's such fun to see them all,
Winter, summer, spring, and fall;
One by one I watch them peep
Till at last I fall asleep.

Clara Bell Thurston

THE FRIENDLY DARK

The friendly dark just fills my room
   When I'm in bed at night;

It creeps on tiptoe all around
   To take the place of light.

Barbara Hanna

MY STAR

In a sky of black velvet
The silver stars shine.
I think I'll choose one
And pretend it is mine.
I'll choose one that twinkles
And winks down at me;
Then snug in my bed every
Night I shall see
My very own star shining
Far overhead,
And winking good night to me,
Curled up in bed.

Marion Kennedy

Enjoying and Creating Poetry

Follow these suggestions for using the poetry in this book and for helping children appreciate poets and their work. Reproducible pages will encourage original verse writing. Add your ideas to these and let your students enjoy and create!

Using the Poems in This Book

The most important use of the poems in this book is, of course, to read and enjoy them as literature. The way the words invoke an image or word picture, the mood each poem creates, the idea a poet wants us to think about—these are some of the essential elements of poetry. As you and your class read a poem together, talk about these elements and how they make us see something in a new way. Once you've read *Autumn* (page 12), for example, will you ever again walk through brown, crunchy leaves and not think of cornflakes? You don't always have to dissect a poem. On a dreary, rainy day, read aloud Langston Hughes's *April Rain Song* (page 75) with no comment and let each student think his or her own thoughts on rain.

1. When you want to help pupils understand specific aspects of literature, poetry has excellent examples. Start with some of the many forms of picturesque speech.
Onomatopoeia—the use of a word whose

sound suggests the sense. Read *My Drum* (page 149) and ask pupils to listen to the taps. Can they hear the sounds of the drum? Other good examples of onomatopoeia can be found in *Lawn-Mower, Vacuum Cleaner,* or *Our Washing Machine* (pages 143, 146).

Personification—the assignment of human qualities to an animate or inanimate object. Many verses in this book use personification. Some of the best examples are in *Dreams* (page 136), *Things to Do If You Are a Subway* (page 139), and *Passing by the Junkyard* (page 147).

Simile—the comparison of two unlike things, usually using the words *like* or *as*. Ask pupils to find the similes in *Smoke* (page 147) and *The Subway Train* (page 151).

Metaphor—an implied comparison of dissimilar things, not using the words *like* or *as*. These verses contain metaphors: *Toaster* (page 148), *An Explanation of the Grasshopper* (page 125), *The Ladies* (page 121), *Aeroplane* (page 107).

Building ideas and sentences to reach a climax is another literary form. Read *Lincoln Spoke* (page 61) and see how his life and the poem move progressively to a climax.

Children can appreciate the word pictures in verse of the seasons and holidays. Help them capture the mood of a snowy day (page 47), the turbulence of a storm on the Great Lakes (page 128), the spookiness of Halloween (pages 19-24), the joy of Hanukkah (pages 34-35), and the enthusiasm of a patriotic parade (page 104).

Poems can help children understand personal feelings and problems. After reading *Exactly Right* (page 132) and *Everybody Says* (page 131), they realize that others have been in the same predicament. And who has not had the feelings expressed in the companion poems *Brothers* and *Sisters* (page 133)?

2. There are many other ways to use poetry; let it be the basis for class or school programs.

Choral readings make effective programs to perform for parents or classmates. Select a rather long verse and divide lines among various groups—high voices, low voices, solo parts, entire chorus. The Martin Luther King verse (page 54), for example, would be an effective choral speaking rendition. Or select several of the Hanukkah verses (pages 34-35), with small groups or individuals reading different ones to create a Hanukkah performance.

For special effects, the class can set a verse to music, or you can select appropriate music as background while pupils are reading. Some verses lend themselves well to pantomime (*A Snowball*, page 53) or creative movement (*Signs of Spring*, page 82).

Some poems can start pupils thinking about creative dramatic productions. Make your Christmas celebrations more original with dramatized scenes inspired by *Christmas Is a Warm Thing* (page 37). For an end-of-school program, dramatize scenes of summer fun, based on poems about the seashore, the playground, camping, traveling, and so on. Or devise a program on our nation's heroes and heroines, using the poems here plus those in other anthologies.

3. Use poetry to introduce a unit or special project. Primary grades often have a unit on getting ready for winter. Use pages 16-17 and 49-50 to introduce such a project.

Begin a transportation study with a discussion of some of the poems on pages 150-152 and the story of the Wright brothers (page 36).

The "Words, words, words" poems (pages 160-163) will be especially interesting when doing some language arts activities. An entire lesson on word usage can be developed from *See How They Run* (page 160).

Units on map study, insects, air and weather, city life, and more can easily get their motivation from the poems here.

4. Use poetry as the inspiration for all kinds of creative-writing endeavors.

The poetry-writing section at the end of this chapter talks about special kinds of verse writing, but as you and your pupils read and enjoy a poem, you might suggest students create their own in the same format. Start with *Words* (page 161), for example, and write a class poem of fast words, slow words, short words, long words, big, little, high, low, and so on. Once they get started, pupils can go on indefinitely.

Or talk about *Skyscrapers* (page 141). They don't scrape skies, of course, but many things don't do what their names imply. Use the examples in *Happy April Fool's Day Verbs* (page 71) plus others the class thinks of for individual verses about these tricky words.

After looking at some of the "Everyday things" poems (pages 143-148), have a brainstorming session to list as many ordinary objects as the class can think of. Let each student select one as the topic for some creative writing. They might start with some of these:

nails and the things they hold together

a ballpoint pen and the immortal words it writes

a frying pan and the food it has cooked for four generations

a returnable soft-drink bottle and its adventure each time it leaves the bottling plant

5. Use poetry to inspire art activities. The autumn and October poems (pages 12-14) will set the mood for interesting watercolor and wash paintings. The bright oranges, browns, yellows, and reds of autumn leaves make interesting collage and abstract designs. On a restless afternoon, create a quick class mural to illustrate *October Is for Me* (page 14) or *Pirate Wind* (page 13).

Halloween is a good subject for scratch-crayon drawings. Have children use crayons to color paper completely with bright fall colors, then cover with solid black. Display a verse that invites spooky pictures; children scratch off the black to make a scene that the poem suggests.

Chalk drawings lend themselves well to winter pictures. Again display one or more verses, especially those about snow and ice, and let pupils interpret the mood with pastel chalk. Or turn to the winter verses on outdoor fun (pages 51-53). Pupils can paint bright tempera figures playing a winter sport. When the paint dries, they fill in the background with pastel chalk to depict a snowy, blowy day.

Abstract paintings in stylized shapes done with tempera may be the result after reading and talking about some of the spring flower poetry (pages 87-90).

Often a poem can be part of a poster to announce a coming event. Create posters to advertise Children's Book Week, National Li-

brary Week, a Halloween party, a pet parade, a Memorial Day observance. Or create a wall display in the hall to remind everyone about Martin Luther King, Jr.,'s birthday, Veterans Day, United Nations Week, Flag Day, and so on. Use a poem or part of one as the focal point, with pertinent facts and class drawings mounted around it.

6. Use poetry to develop bulletin boards. Start with a welcome-to-school board. Print one of the "Back to school" poems (pages 7-10) and center it on the board. On the first day, ask pupils to illustrate it with a decorative border, original drawings, or pictures cut from magazines. This activity not only saves you time, but gets your class involved immediately in the practice of creating its own displays.

With the right poem, a seasonal bulletin board will almost make itself. Write a poem in large letters and mount on the board. Let each pupil add one thing to illustrate his or her ideas about it—a drawing, an original poem, a magazine picture, a recommendation for a book on the topic, a personal account of the celebration at home, and so on.

But use poems for other topics, too. If you are having a spring project on growing things, for example, use *Food's Found* (page 148) to create an unusual bulletin board. Divide it horizontally into three areas, each area representing a verse of the poem, and have pupils draw in the foods mentioned in the poem. Be sure not to forget the peanut.

Use *Who?* (page 33) as the focus of a display on tracks. Children in rural areas will be able to draw examples of those they have seen around their homes or on their way to school.

One of the seasonal poems can start a bulletin board of newspaper pictures, stories, or advertisements of signs of winter, signs of spring, and so on. Put a low table in front of the board for such objects as abandoned birds' nests and colored leaves, or budding pussy willows and a blooming crocus.

Personal drawings may be inspired by some of the "All about me" poems (pages 130-132). Use one of the "Family and friends" poems (pages 133-135) to encourage displays of family groups. Cut sheets of paper in a stylized house shape for pupils to fill with family members. Remember, a family is any group of people living and loving together. Label the board "Our Class Families."

Summer can be an exciting time for some children, a dull one for those who can't think of a thing to do. Create an end-of-year bulletin board that lists many kinds of summer activities in your area, using some of the summer vacation poems to illustrate it. Or create a class book of summer poems with a listing of things to do. Duplicate a copy for each child to take home to refer to during the summer recess.

Selecting Poems for Personal Enjoyment

Poetry is a many-splendored thing. Some qualities that make it so include its timelessness and historic import, its folklore and customs revealed through oral tradition, its value as fun and entertainment, its inspirational qualities as a touchstone for character and ideals, its revelation of beauty, its gift to the imaginative power of childhood, its power to invoke laughter, its bequest of the glory and wonder of words, and its use as a solace to comfort the fearful child in a world of hostility.

Today's child will appreciate good poetry if he or she is fortunate enough to have an encounter with poetry of value. As there is a right book for each child, so there is the right poem for each child. Unfortunately, many adults look back with nostalgia at the poetry of their childhood and offer outmoded, stereotyped poems to children. A mother remembers excerpts from *Snowbound* or *Evangeline*, for example, and urges her fifth-grade daughter to read it. After struggling through the concepts and language, she looks with aversion on all poetry. Help pupils learn to enjoy poetry by choosing poems they can understand and appreciate. Use these guidelines by Ruth Kearney Carlson.

Rhythm and language

Readers respond emotionally to poetry that has melodious rhythms. A poem offers a sense of patterned sound, a regular repetition of beat or swing occurring at regular intervals. Young children do not need tedious lessons in scansion to enjoy and interpret the rhythm of a poem, but sometimes youngsters feel that all poetry must rhyme. Listeners who become too absorbed with rhyme are inclined to select and write meaningless jingles. In selecting poems for children, present a variety of poetry styles—verse of conventional patterns, free verse, blank verse, and even a few examples of Oriental styles of syllabic verse.

Select poetry that has an unhackneyed use of language. Sometimes a poet uses a particular word that is just the right one and raises a poem above the commonplace. Good poetry introduces the child-reader to some of the most wondrous words and ideas in the English language. The poet's imaginative eye sees beauty in many things—the crystal clear snowflake, the scarlet dash of color in a blackbird's wing, or the rough ridge of a firm footprint. Beauty lies in the eye of the beholder, but the skilled poet helps the child to observe minute particles of experience in a way that helps the eye to become more alerted to the chiseled shape of an emerald or the spherical, globular curve of a drop of oil.

Poems of varying interests

To meet the individualized interests of pupils, you will need poems in a variety of subjects. Create interest inventories (perhaps sports, nature, pets, history, family, music, things mechanical) and help children to select poems related to their particular interests. For instance, hundreds of children's poems have been written about birds, but also some excellent ones have been created about snails and snakes, starfish and spiders, and even about toads.

Poems of laughter

Children need laughing time to counteract fears and worries, and humorous poetry offers a chance to laugh and giggle. Choose poems to help the child laugh at ridiculous lines and situations. Laughter is therapeutic, but funny poems also help the reader to note the inventiveness of poets in the use of our language. Puns, juxtaposed situations, onomatopoetic words—all help the reader to enlarge his or her vocabulary and to manipulate phrases and words. The child can enjoy the bantering humor of the ridiculous lines and may become curious about words and their constructions.

Poems of comfort

The world of the present is cluttered with difficulties and grief; the modern child is assaulted by noisy freeways, monstrous-sized jet planes, and visions of dark-mushroomed nuclear holocausts. Sometimes a well-meaning stranger or an oversolicitous parent also becomes a threat and a nightmare. An appropriate poem may help a child take care of "Myself and I," and face these many problems. Such poems are private things, bits of verse to be treasured personally.

Poems of fancy

Some of the poems selected for children should be fanciful. Romanticizing about seemingly impossible situations and people opens up a world of experience and expands the possibilities of imaginative thinking. All peoples of the world have conjured up fanciful creatures—goblins, fairies, elves, leprechauns. The child of today must take time to dream, and dreaming will lead him or her into the world of fancy.

Poems of inspiration and ideals

Some poetry should be selected that raises the aspirations and ideals of childhood, but poems of this type should not be too moralistic.

Holiday poetry is designed for use in the celebration of important days and the lives of famous patriots of our country. Teachers should use a card file or expandable loose-leaf binder to collect samples of good poetry that inspires rather than bores. Children will gain a different viewpoint of the traditions and history of the United States after reading good poems about famous Americans and poems that reveal the pioneer spirit of their forefathers.

Life does have "loveliness to sell," and children will truly enjoy poetry that is selected to meet the need of each individual self in the relevance of the world today.

The Poetry Center

True appreciation and love of poetry can only come about when children have many opportunities to read, enjoy, and create their own verse. Make it available to them at all times with a poetry center that will provide students with frequent poetry encounters. But change the center's appearance and your approach to poetry often so the encounters don't become dull and old hat. The following ideas, adapted from articles in INSTRUCTOR magazine, will ensure that you will always have some new and exciting poetry activities to motivate your group.

Is today poetry day?

When was the last time one of your pupils walked up to you and asked, "Is today poetry day?" Well, there are ways to arouse that kind of fascination for poetry among children. Some of the successful ones extend poetry into movement, art, and writing.

Movement Begin with a little mystery. If you are introducing a poem about fireflies, for example, ask questions like these: Can you think of an insect that is seen when it is warm? Only at night? That has its own light that blinks on and off as it flies around?

After the class has identified the insect, discuss the appropriateness of the names *lightning bug* and *firefly*. Then read the poem. Next have the class do activities based on firefly movements, such as the following.

Make yourself as small as you can—as small as a firefly. Stand up and make light walking steps—as light as a firefly. Put your arms straight out from your side and pretend they are wings that are warming up for flying. Move them very slowly in little circles, then faster and faster. Using firefly steps and whirling wings, move around as though you are flying outside.

You have just been caught and placed in a jar. Reach out and touch the glass sides and bottom. Someone has removed the lid. Fly away, fly away!

Art Collages can serve as excellent art activities after reading poems about color. If a particular poem centers, for instance, on the color red, have your kids identify a variety of objects that are red. Photographs and drawings of red objects can then be cut from magazines and pasted on red construction paper and the collages displayed on the classroom bulletin board. In a similar vein, faces can be made on paper plates and displayed after sharing poems about faces.

Writing It's natural to encourage kids to write after hearing or reading thought-provoking poems. Poems that involve accomplishment are particularly good for stimulating children to think and write about a time they really felt proud. Kids will come up with items like: "I really felt proud when I learned to swim, to stand on my head, to ride my bike, to climb a fence," and so on.

After hearing poems involving the word *quiet,* one class wrote about other quiet things: "As quiet as a picture hanging; as quiet as a flea; as quiet as a car not running; as quiet as a flower growing."

Then the kids wrote about the opposite: noisy things. "As noisy as a hog squealing; as noisy as a class yelling; as noisy as a dog barking; as noisy as a waterfall."

Extending poetry through movement, art, and writing elicits enthusiastic responses from children. Creativity, ingenuity, and individuality are fostered, while enjoyment and appreciation of poetry are developed. So select a poem, try some extending activities, and remember that the sky's the limit!
Carol J. Fisher and Margaret A. Natarella

The unexpected
Vary the way you present a poem. Have a puppet say it; tape-record it with sound effects; sing it, making up a tune (some are already set to music); illustrate the action with flannel board characters; let children dramatize as you read; make appropriate shadow figures; display objects mentioned; provide props so children can identify with characters.

Illustrate a poetry bulletin board with a variety of media: real bark and green tissue make a tree; melted crayon and glitter become a fireworks display; painted cardboard strips form a house; cornflakes and water build into a snowdrift; starched cloth on cutouts of kittens turns into calico cats.   *Beth Norton*

Poet-tree
Construct a poet-tree. Use a dry branch from any tree or bush and mount on a wooden stand. Cut poems from children's magazines and mount on 3″ × 5″ cards, or type poems on the cards. A paper clip bent into an S hook becomes a quick hanger with which to festoon the tree with a bit of verse. Filing poems by month, topic, and season makes it easy for a class member to freshen the tree with new verses. Children will eagerly await these new offerings. It is not long before the tree will also bear fruit of the children's own creative efforts.   *Dennis C. Loggins*

Mobiles
Make poetry mobiles to emphasize seasonal and holiday poetry. Create a simple mobile, using paper shapes that portray the season—leaves for fall, flowers for spring, tree ornaments for Christmas, flags for Flag Day, and so on. As pupils find appropriate verses they like, they write them on the shapes. Strive for a huge class mobile, or encourage individual ones.

Poetry collection
Often favorite poems are found in library books which must be returned and then, of

course, the poems are gone. Or even if the books remain, pupils are likely to forget which book contains which poem. But put a typewriter in your poetry center and watch the excitement. (You can probably borrow one for a few weeks if you don't have one.)

Develop a file of favorite poems by having children type them on large file cards. Purchase a metal file or adapt a shoe box and appoint a committee to devise a method of classifying and filing poems. Because mistakes in typing often lead to retyping, many poems will be memorized inadvertently. Spelling will take on real importance, and poetry forms will become as familiar as prose forms. The file will be a treasured part of your classroom all year, with poems being added to it continuously.

Marilyn Chrisman Fais

Poetry picture books

Try a poetry-illustrating project with your upper graders. Let each student select any poem he or she likes from any book, magazine, or newspaper and illustrate the lines with magazine pictures. Pictures should portray what the student feels the corresponding lines mean. Allow ample time for browsing; often a seemingly unrelated picture will suddenly give new meaning to a line or stanza.

Create simple booklets with one picture and its corresponding line or lines on a page. Chances are good that by the time the booklet is completed, the poem will be memorized and become a permanent part of a pupil's experience.

Dolores Splaingard

Personal anthologies

At holiday time, suggest your middle and upper graders make personal verse anthologies. Each student designs a cover around a holiday symbol and cuts it out. Inside sheets are cut to match and everything is stapled together. Original and published verses are written on the pages, each child selecting and writing his or her favorite choices. Make sure booklets go home to be shared with family and friends.

Jean-Marie Welch

Poetry Day

October 15 is Poetry Day. Use it as a good excuse for developing a class program based on favorite poems. Selections can be determined by class vote. Discuss varied and interesting ways of sharing the poems, but let children decide for themselves what they want to do. No one need memorize a poem but many will know their selections before the program. These ideas will start you on the way to featuring the chosen poems.

Cut a large shape of the poem's principal character (perhaps a jack-o'-lantern) and pin it to a sheet. Light from a filmstrip projector shining behind the sheet will make it appear in silhouette. The picture will hold the visual attention of the class while poem is read.

When using a poem with a regular rhyming scheme, invite audience participation. Put the rhyming words on a portable chalkboard. Read the first line of a couplet and call on a student to supply the needed rhyming word; then read the second line, and so on.

The whole group might recite a poem while one or two people pantomime it.

Project class drawings of zoo animals with the overhead projector while individuals read appropriate poems.

Bette Jacobs

A living process

Make poetry a living process your children can experience. What better way for children to live poetry than to read the printed word, building their awareness of suitability and juxtaposition of words, their understanding of the development of this art form, and then, with guidance, their writing of it.

Don't begin with a specific verse form, but rather a written response to a particular idea. Start with something as innocent on the surface as *What is (success, silence, blue)?* In this type of poem, each line is a varying length and rhythm and is a statement unto itself. However, as you write the first poem with the help of your students, the rhythm which is inbred in all of us will probably begin to surface. If it doesn't appear, there's no harm done. No poet begins with meter, but with a theme, an idea, an image.

Silence is being alone.
Silence is the wood at night.
It is a forest after a fire.
Silence is an empty room.
It is a house for sale.

These lines are humble beginnings. But once the students have experienced the thrill of creating for themselves in an open form, more stylized modes of expression can be experimented with, to house each child's own theme, idea, or image.

There are many poetic forms available with which to create expression. Among them are the triangular triplet, a three-line verse whose lines can be read in any order, and the diamante, a diamond-shaped contrast poem. Here are two examples.

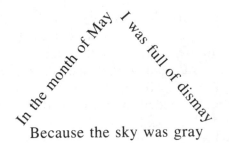

Because the sky was gray

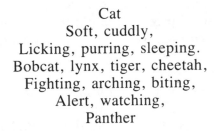

To those of you who fear to stumble along with this activity, listen to the unguarded chatter of your students to determine their interests. Then choose poems depicting historical events, literary achievements, or geographical scenes. Introduce them into your lessons as a natural part of your exposition, and then gradually take the time to consider them on their merits. The study of this art form requires infinite patience, a great deal of faith, and much loving care. It will, however, both teach and delight by harmonizing knowing and feeling.

Lorna H. Haworth

Concrete poetry

Children will have fun with concrete poetry—poetry that is written in the shape of its subject. Demonstrate this intriguing form of art-literature by writing this poem, *The Kite*, on the board.

```
Fly
and soar                    sky
dip and dive,                 e
Chase the wind                 h
  as if alive.                  t
  The dancing                    h
  kite can                        c
   float                          u
   and                           o
   fly                          t
    u                         o
    n                       t
     til it seems
```

Next have the class work together to create a concrete poem, using one of these titles: *The Worm, The Ball, The Circle*. Once students are comfortable writing concrete poetry, using simple shapes, encourage them to make a list of familiar seasonal designs—tree, star, leaf, heart, and so on. Then each student chooses a shape and writes a poem in that shape.

Children love the challenge of concrete poetry—it offers the chance to consider the relationship of words to ideas and shapes. And the holiday season is a perfect time to get your class in shape.

Florence L. Morgan

Two-word poetry

What is two-word poetry? It's word conservation, especially emphasizing the use of two descriptive words per line as a teaching technique in poetry. Your students will become avid poetry writers after an experience with this technique.

Here's what I did. First I told my children, ''We are going to write a new kind of poetry. Each line will have only two words in it. We have to choose our words carefully so each line makes a complete picture. Then by combining several two-word pictures, anyone should be able to visualize what we have described. Now, what do you suggest we should write about?''

Silence.

''Very well. Suppose we select something in school.''

A hand shot up and a voice said, ''What about you?''

''Me?'' I said, in pretended surprise. ''Well, all right. But remember,'' I cautioned, ''you must use words you really think describe me." I was now open to fourth-grade honesty and started to jot down tactful, ego-building phrases on the chalkboard.

Our teacher
Very tall
Very thin
Weak eyes
Thick glasses

"Let's backtrack," I said. "We need another word picture in here. How would someone reading this know whether your teacher is a man or a woman?"

"Write down a woman," they said.

"What kind of woman?" I asked.

"Skinny woman," was the giggling reply.

"How tall?" I continued.

"Very tall," they repeated.

"Not very," I said. "What's the tallest thing you can think of?"

"A giraffe!" We continued in this manner and by the end of our first session I began to emerge as:

Our teacher	Dyed scalp
Skinny woman	Red strings
Mrs. Schmidlin	Goose neck
Giraffe tall	Ichabod arms
Wire thin	Whale bottom
Blind eyes	Funny clothes
Bug glasses	Old-fashioned
Elephant nose	Knee skirts
Mean mouth	Pointed shoes

My ego was slightly deflated but soon began to rise again when several children asked if they could start writing their own poems. Seconds later the questions began. How long does it have to be? Long enough to describe your subject. Should it rhyme? No. What's another word for *little?* At this point I reminded the class that if they wanted bigger words they should use our dictionaries, encyclopedias, or beginning thesaurus. The stampede to the reference books was on. . . .

Apart from encouraging the use of reference sources, two-word poetry provides opportunity for word inventions, unusual go-togethers, and rhyming quickies.

Lake high,	Sheep eat,
Lake low,	Sheep drink,
Lakes come,	Sheep sleep,
Lakes go.	Sheep stink.

Given complete freedom, children will write about anything. If you would like to try two-word poetry, follow one rule—use two words only; three destroy careful word choice. But everything else is flexible. Add the excitement and fun of two-word poetry to your language program. *Lois Nelsen Schmidlin*

Patchwork poetry

Creating a patchwork poem is an exciting approach to poetic composition. Children will learn a variety of skills and have fun, too.

Most children like nothing better than cutting pictures out of magazines. Armed with the proper scissors and outdated magazines, almost any child can become a poet by using words and phrases from the printed page.

Looking for the right words can benefit reading skills, too. Let students first go through the magazines and find words or phrases that appeal to their senses. Where the age group indicates it, point out words with graphic appeal and introduce subject words, object words, and words that modify. Pupils should cut out any words or groups of words that catch the eye and have special meaning for them. No need to try to fit them into any particular meaning right away—just browse through the pages and clip out whatever appeals. Then have students take a large, white sheet of drawing paper, or similar paper, and start to arrange the words and pictures on it.

Seasonal words are excellent to get a poem going or to pull one together. *Summer, autumn, spring,* and *winter* can become the poem's title, its first line, or an ending. Suggest students keep rearranging the words as inspiration moves them. Suddenly, the poem will begin to take shape. Then they will discover they need more words to complete a thought in the poem. The search through the magazines will resume. More ideas will be triggered. Urge them to keep clipping and arranging. Maybe a second or a third poem will begin to present itself. Students should put these words and phrases together before the elusive inspiration vanishes. Be sure they don't paste anything until they are sure this is the way they want the poem to appear finally. Once arranged in patterns that seem artistic or that balance well or that suggest the shape of the poem, everything can be pasted down on the paper.

Suitable illustrations can also be gleaned from magazine pages and used to accompany the poem. Or reverse the process and choose an illustration to inspire word selection. Individuals can work on their own, or the class could select a full-page illustration and then pick out the words that best suit the mood of the picture.

Perhaps someone has found a picture that goes well with the title. In the example here, the picture of the birch trees seemed to "belong" to the title, *Summer*. The variety of print sizes of birch trees seems to scatter on the page much as the birches are scattered in the woods in varying shapes and sizes. And the words now point up the way to a new discovery—a yellow daisy. From the multiple arrangement of birch trees to the discovery of the single yellow daisy, the journey through the poem is identical to the journey through the birch trees. It seems, upon finding it, that the daisy becomes as large and important as the birch trees themselves. Thus the daisy illustration is large and is arranged at the end of the poem like a huge exclamation point!

Patchwork poems can be an in-school project or a take-home project. Making one's book of patchwork poems might also be a term project. After searching a few magazines for suitable expressive words and ideas, the student will have a much better concept of what it takes to make a poem. It also will give him or her added respect for poets and poetry writing as well as a greater knowledge of the value of the right word for the right expression of an idea. Give patchwork poetry a try.

Lorraine Ellis Harr

Writing Formal Verse

Our first responsibility as pipers of poetry is to help children enjoy the rhythm, melody, and story of a poem. Students gradually can be introduced to the more sophisticated elements of meter, rhyme pattern, and stanza—but only after they have had many experiences with beginning poetry forms such as the two-word poetry and triangular triplets described in the previous section. Following are some of the more formal forms of verse to introduce to your students when they are ready.

Haiku Originally called "hokko," or "starting verse," haiku is an effective pattern for expressing trains of thought and strains of feeling. It consists of a few words that carry a great amount of meaning. The economy of expression; the single image; and the warmth, vigor, and simplicity of this Japanese poetry form give the child opportunity to think, feel, and communicate.

The basic pattern of haiku is simple: it has 17 unrhymed syllables organized into three lines of 5, 7, and 5 syllables. A good haiku verse has a vibrant image and is usually a breath of beauty. This beauty is communicated through the use of concrete images: a blue dragonfly, a bright pepper pod, a croaking frog, or an empty rice bowl. A Japanese haiku poet usually utilizes a seasonal theme. Spring is frequently symbolized through the nightingale, the plum, and the cherry blossom. The cuckoo is a subject of summer poems. The moon often symbolizes autumn.

Use this outline to help develop the haiku concept with your children:

Where (5 syllables)—on the old gnarled limb
What (7 syllables)—a crow above is cawing;
When (5 syllables)—autumn stillness now.

Set the stage for haiku writing by collecting objects from nature for everyone to observe—grasses, weeds, interesting stones, a single, perfect flower—plus bright colored pictures of butterflies, birds, beetles, and so on. Ask each child to write a brief paragraph describing one of the items. He or she then picks out some of the key words to create three lines of 5, 7, and 5 syllables, telling the where, what, and when of the object. (The reproducible on page 181 is a good haiku activity.)

Tanka This Oriental verse pattern is really an extension of haiku with a 5, 7, 5, 7, 7 syllabic pattern. In tanka verse, the dominant pause occurs at the end of the third line, but a minor pause may be at the end of any line. Tanka verse may rhyme or not. This good example was written by seventh grader Kenneth.

The sky at sunset
Is so wonderful to view
Golden pink and rose
But . . . next morning I now see
A sky as clear as water.

Sijo This verse pattern was developed in Korea. Its structure has three lines with 14 to 16 syllables to a line, but each line can be divided into parts with a pause at the end of the first part. The sijo can express any emotion—gaiety, sadness, grief, or fear. It originally was sung at court to the tune of a lute. Many sijo verses are about nature or use symbols of nature. Often things that are unlike will be compared: mountains opposed to sea, the sky to earth, or the sun to rain. When translated into English, this verse form appears in six short lines. Here's an example by student William Sullivan.

What a gloomy, snowy night.
Dull and moody, all the way.
The ship's crew are all in fright
The choppy waves roll off the coast
In the galley pots are rattling
Storm-stopped ships sail on their way.

Cinquain This verse form, developed by Adelaide Crapsey, is an offspring of haiku. Part of the word comes from the French and Spanish word for "five" and refers to the fact that the cinquain has five lines. Cinquain verse does not rhyme but has a set number of syllables per line. Each line also has a specific purpose or meaning.

Line 1 (2 syllables)—states the title
Line 2 (4 syllables)—describes the title
Line 3 (6 syllables)—expresses an action
Line 4 (8 syllables)—expresses a feeling
Line 5 (2 syllables)—another word for the title

This cinquain by Danny is a good example of what children can do.

My pups
Playful fellows
Chewing my father's shoes
And all they get from me is love
Young mutts

Use the reproducible on page 182 to help your children write cinquains.

Meter, rhyme, stanza As children become more sophisticated readers and creators of poetry, they can become acquainted with certain terminology such as meter, rhyme, and stanza.

Meter refers to the rhythm pattern of a poetic line. It results from the syllabic word pattern measured by accent and repetition. Such words as *preserve, enthuse, apart* are two-syllable words. Each word has one accented syllable and one unaccented syllable. An unaccented syllable is called a feminine syllable and is designated by a rocker (⌣). An accented syllable is called masculine and is marked with a dash (—). Sometimes an accented syllable is indicated by the accent symbol (').

The foot is a poetic term for a grouping of one stressed syllable and one or two unstressed syllables. English poetry has four common types of metrical feet; the types vary according to where the accent falls.

Iambic foot—accent falls on second syllable (dĕ light')

Trochaic foot—accent is on the first syllable (moth' ĕr)

Anapestic foot—two unaccented syllables are followed by one accented one (ĭn cŏm plete')

Dactylic foot—one accented syllable is followed by two unaccented ones (tel' ĕ grăm)

Occasionally, to vary the rhythm, a substitute foot is used. One kind of substitute is *spondaic*—two long or accented syllables (hum' drum'). Another kind is the *pyrrhic foot*—two short or unaccented syllables (ŏf thĕ). Most English lines of poetry contain one to eight feet.

Although this type of writing may be too advanced for most children, some might be challenged to try one or two lines, in one of the meters described above. (See page 183.)

Rhyme helps to give shape or form to verse and to bind the lines together. The listener's ear is expectantly attuned to rhyme and waits for the rhyming sound. Usually, the ear does not carry the sound of rhyme over more than three intervening unrhymed lines, so poets frequently create verses which rhyme somewhere within that limit. Rhyming lines must appear natural and seem spontaneous.

The rhymed couplet is the simplest form of poetic stanza and consists of two rhyming lines. First-grade children easily create couplets and chant them as they skip along or jump rope. The rhyme scheme of a rhymed couplet is indicated by a/a. Lines of a couplet may be any metrical pattern or length which reinforces the thought. (See page 184.)

The quatrain is a four-line verse pattern which may have any rhythm. It has any one of several rhyming schemes: aabb, in which lines 1 and 2 rhyme, and lines 3 and 4 rhyme; abcb, where the second and fourth lines rhyme and the other two do not; abab; and abba. A closing rhyme usually binds the four lines together. If the last line does not rhyme with any previous line, the stanza loses unity. A stanza of eight lines is usually two quatrains.

After some experiences with couplets, suggest pupils look for examples of the different rhyming schemes of quatrains. Then create a class poem using one of these schemes. Start by choosing a subject or dramatic scene. Then decide on the time of day, the weather, the exact place, a situation, and so on. Perhaps the subject is a skier; the weather is cold but the sun is shining; it is early morning; the skier is on the ski lift; and so on. Give children a chance to think for a few minutes, then write proposed lines on the chalkboard. After all who want to have suggested lines, let the class select those that seem to go together and work them in to a selected rhyming scheme. If the images are vivid, the poem will almost write itself. After the class has written its poem, give pupils time to create their own on this same subject. (See page 185.)

Sonnet A sonnet is a lyric form of 14 lines usually written in iambic pentameter (five iambic feet). The form originated in Italy and is built on two ideas, one related to the other. The first eight lines are called the octave; this usually develops the principal idea, presents a picture, or makes an assertion. The final six lines are the sestet, which presents the solution, a comment, or an application of the idea in the octave. The sonnet's rhyme scheme is abbaabba/cdcdcd. The sonnets of Shakespeare and other Elizabethan writers have a different rhyme scheme: abab/cdcd/efef/gg.

Limerick The limerick has five anapestic lines. Lines 1, 2, and 5 have three feet, lines 3 and 4, two. The rhyme pattern is aabba.

> There once was an Ichthyosaurus
> Who lived when the earth was all porous,
> But he fainted with shame
> When he first heard his name,
> And departed a long time before us.

Read several limericks to your pupils so they can hear the rhythmical style and discover the story pattern. (Be sure to read them to yourself first; the limerick form seems to lend itself to risqué topics or situations.) Start children writing their own limericks by giving them a first and a third line. Pupils then have the two rhyming words and can more easily complete the limerick.

Adapted from Poetry for Today's Child *by Ruth Kearney Carlson (© 1972, 1968, Instructor Publications, Inc., New York, N.Y.)*

Reproducible 1—LET'S WRITE HAIKU

Japanese haiku is a three-line poem about nature. The first and third lines have 5 syllables, the second line has 7. Do these prewriting exercises first, then try your hand at haiku.

What is your favorite season? _____

Write something special about this season's weather. _____

_____

_____

Give an action of a bird or animal in this season. _____

_____

_____

Talk about a flower or other plant that grows during this season. __

_____

_____

_____

Now pick one of these topics: weather, bird, animal, or flower. Write your haiku, telling where it is, what it is, when it is happening. Be sure you keep to the number of syllables written at the end of each line.

_____5

_____7

_____5

Reproducible 2—CREATING A CINQUAIN

A cinquain is a five-line verse that talks about one topic. Each line has its own special purpose and a particular number of syllables. First do these prewriting exercises.

1. Name a favorite animal. _____

2. Write some words that describe it. _____

_____

3. Tell one thing that it does. _____

_____

4. Describe how you feel about it. _____

_____

5. Give another name for your animal. _____

Use the words above to create your cinquain. The word you wrote on line 1 will go on the first line of your poem. The words on line 2 will be used for the second line, and so on. Check to make sure the lines have the correct number of syllables. The numbers at the end of each line will remind you.

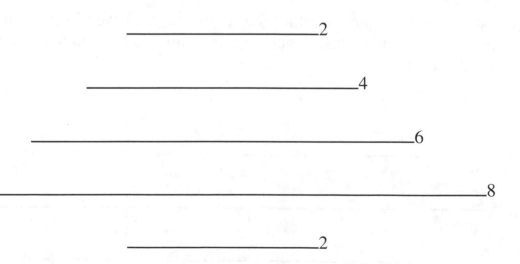

Reproducible 3—WRITING IN METER

Writing phrases and sentences in metric form is a challenge. But if you use these ideas, you can be successful.

Name a party you attended or would like to attend. _____

Who was there (relatives, friends)? _____

_____

What was the reason for the party (holiday, birthday)? _____

_____

What did you do (play games, talk, sing)? _____

_____

What did you eat?_____

Where did the party take place (someone's home, park)? _____

Now turn some of your answers into phrases that have these meters. Good luck!

Iambic meter ∪/   ∪/   ∪/   ∪/

_____

Trochaic meter /∪   /∪   /∪   /∪

_____

Anapestic meter ∪∪/   ∪∪/   ∪∪/   ∪∪/

_____

Dactylic meter /∪∪   /∪∪   /∪∪   /∪∪

_____

Reproducible 4—TRY COUPLETS

Do you like colors? Think of a favorite one. Put its name in the blank below. Then tell why you like it. Make the last word in the second line rhyme with the color you named in the first line. There are a few rhyming clues below, but try to think of your own.

One of my favorite colors is _____.

_____

_____.

You've written a rhyming couplet.

Now think of a color you don't like. Add a rhyming line that tells why.

A color I'm not very fond of is _____.

_____

_____.

You've written another couplet.
Use your imagination to create a third couplet. Write about another color or pick any topic you'd like, maybe your pet or an imaginary animal.

_____

_____

red	blue	green	yellow	pink	brown
bed	grew	mean	mellow	rink	frown
head	few	seen	fellow	mink	clown
fed	flue	lean	Jell-O	stink	town
sled	true	jean	cello	link	down

Reproducible 5—QUATRAINS ARE FUN

A quatrain is a four-line verse. It can rhyme any way you wish—aabb, abab, abcb, abba, or aaaa. Do these prewriting exercises first.

Name someone playing a sport. _____

Tell this person's size. _____

_____

Describe the look on his or her face. _____

_____

How is he or she dressed? _____

_____

What is the weather? _____

What is about to happen? _____

_____

Will the person be successful at what he is trying to do? _____

From your answers to these questions, select sentences to create a quatrain. Use whatever rhyme scheme you want.

_____

_____

_____

_____

Title index

Author index